FACEBOOK ADVERTISING TRENDS

— AND —

STRATEGIES

FOR E-COMMERCE

2020 EDITION

Printed in the USA

First Edition

ISBN: 978-0-6484407-2-7

Cover Design: Studio 1 Design and Jek Tibayan

Interior Design and Layout: Swish Design

To my fellow entrepreneurs that are driven to accept nothing but the best for themselves and their loved ones. This book is dedicated to you for always giving 110%.

CONTENTS

FACEBOOK
ADVERTISING
TRENDS
— AND —
STRATEGIES
FOR E-COMMERCE

2020 EDITION

JOSH MARSDEN, MBA

INTRODUCTION

Welcome to Facebook Advertising Trends and Strategies For E-Commerce, 2020 Edition!

Congrats on taking the first action towards using and maximizing what Facebook and Instagram Advertising can do for your E-Commerce business here in 2020! You are about to embark on a powerful journey through some incredible strategies that some of the world's best advertisers are going to share with you. It takes a commitment to constant education to stay ahead. The moment you stop learning, you stop growing. Yet, here you are with a powerful book in your hands to put you ahead of trends happening right now with Facebook and Instagram Advertising in 2020. Are you ready to make 2020 your best year yet in business? Keep reading, be the best student that you can be, and you will.

My name is Josh Marsden and I'm the author of the *Facebook Advertising Trends and Strategies* Series. Back in early 2013, I was at a crossroads. I had just made some major changes to my personal and professional life. Namely, I left a successful career in a successful fortune 500 company in Phoenix, Arizona to work at a software company in Chandler, Arizona called Infusionsoft. After nearly a year, exceeding my performance goals at 108%, I was let go.

Luckily, during my time at Infusionsoft, I had picked up fairly quickly how to use the software. I was always tech-savvy with experience programming in high school and building my own computer for the first time at 18. This gave me a skill that I could use to get business so I dove into entrepreneurship, starting as an Infusionsoft freelancer, to test making money on my own for the first time. In the first 30 days, I was "rich" with $1700 earned from freelance service work. It wasn't much but it gave me the courage to keep moving forward. Then, I received a fairly lucrative job offer that I decided to give a shot.

During the first week, I shared with them that I was a single father and would need to leave at 5 PM 1-3 days throughout the week to pick up my then-3-year-old son from school. They didn't like it. Their culture was all about hustle and working long hours Monday through Friday. After 3 weeks of stringing them along, while coercing their discontentment, they gave me an ultimatum that I would have to change my schedule with my son in order to stay employed.

I had a weekend to decide. I sat down, used a large 9" by 11" drafting pad to brain-dump the good and bad behind the two choices in front of me. Stay at this company and barely have time to be a father but have the security of a paycheck or leave the company, figure out how to build my own company, be there for my son, and have no financial ceiling. As you can imagine, the choice was simple. If you are a family man, like I am, you know how precious your moments as a parent are. I wasn't willing to make this ultimate sacrifice. I believed in myself and knew that I had the ingenuity to figure it all out. This gave me the final kick that I needed to be all-in on entrepreneurship and starting my own company. I never looked back. Now, I'm a serial entrepreneur with a thriving Marketing Agency called CVO Acceleration Marketing Performance Agency that helps E-Commerce companies scale to 7-8 figures using a strategy and process that my team and I developed called The ARM5 Formula. I also coach business owners on how to apply The ARM5 Formula so they can acquire customers profitably, and at scale, with digital advertising through my ARM5 Formula Accelerator and ARM5 Formula Elite Mastermind.

Finally, I also co-own several E-Commerce entities that are scaling month-after-month in various niches.

Most importantly, I've been a present father since I've been able to create a flexible schedule as needed while I handle my responsibilities within my companies. It's the simple things. I've been able to pick up my son from school several times throughout the week. I've been able to train my son as he's become an incredible endurance athlete, running 2 half-marathon by the age of 11. I've been able to coach his basketball teams, between our gym and his school. Although having these activities with him would not have been impossible had I made a different choice back in 2013, it would have made it much more challenging.

If you are reading this and you are just getting started or barely into your entrepreneur journey, stay the course. Life is short. Chances are worth taking. Go all-in and don't look back. Hustle and be the best student that you can be. I've been blessed since 2014, when I finally started to make an effort to network, to have some incredible relationships with other entrepreneurs that continue to support me, challenge me, and inspire me. I've been able to learn from some of the best of the best in online business. You can too. Don't ever lose hope and apply grit to get through the tough times. Just win the mental game consistently, and you'll be set.

My mission is to help you scale your company's success. This book will be powerful for you. Thank you so much for picking up a copy of my book. As I mentioned before, take notes, be the best student that you can be, and dive in.

CHAPTER 1

Staying Ahead of the Curve Takes Action

As business owners, it's our responsibility to our business, staff, investors, partners, and audience to pay attention to trends so we can constantly be adapting. The best, most brightest business owners know this. This is why you see the same leaders year in, year out, in business. The best business owners are constantly adapting their business and marketing strategies to win. When you have an eye for the current trends in your industry, your type of business, and in the world, you stay on the cutting edge and give competitors reasons to sweat your existence.

However, staying ahead of trends and adapting your strategies isn't always easy. For one, you have a business to run and more often than not, you get stuck in it. You run the day to day operations. You hold your team accountable. You work with customers. You work on creating new business development deals. To pause and take the time to consume information about topics related to your business isn't easy. Yet, this is a priority and here you are doing it by picking up a copy of this book.

Competitive innovation is one of the biggest trends that business owners face, in every market. E-Commerce owners especially have to be aware of the threat that competitors can be since online business is a relatively easy business to start and it is constantly changing due to its nature in tech. We are seeing more and more E-Commerce businesses being started every day. Part of this is due to drop-shipping. If you didn't know, drop-shipping is an order fulfillment method that does not require a business to keep products in stock. Instead, after the order is processed by an E-Commerce store, a 3rd-party supplier gets the order and then ships it directly to the consumer. This type of E-Commerce business makes it easy for people to get started in E-Commerce since there's very little up-front capital needed to get started.

The tools to start an E-Commerce company have also contributed to the expansion of E-Commerce leading into 2020. Shopify is leading the charge here with over 500,000 active online E-Commerce stores on the software suite. There's also no signs of Shopify slowing down with a reported 59% growth reported from 2018 to 2019. This tells you that there are going to be more and more people entering into the E-Commerce industry and using Shopify to build their online storefront.

This is why business owners need to be vigilant in their commitment to constantly innovate. You can never be complacent and comfortable. The moment that you are, a scrappy upstart in your industry that's hungry and driven can come into your market and steal a considerable piece of your market share. You don't want this. This is why staying on top of marketing innovation and being the threat as opposed to being threatened is key.

Regulations can also have an effect on your business. Especially regulations in marketing, such as the GDPR regulation that came out in 2019 that caused many businesses to change their marketing approach so they would mitigate their risk to regulators in European markets. If you do business in Europe, on any level, you risk being sued for business-threatening levels of money if you don't comply with GDPR regulations. This is just one example. Another more recent example is Facebook just instituted compliance policies for businesses using Facebook Messenger. Now, businesses have to use Facebook Messenger marketing, through software like ManyChat, Segmate, or Opesta, with respect to these new policies or risk losing this invaluable channel in their marketing mix.

The bottom line is that there are constant competitive threats and changes because of the nature of having a business online. Online business is still a relatively new frontier, although it's getting more mature every single year. Although E-Commerce has been mainly responsible for overall retail sales growth year-after-year over the past few years, in 2019 E-Commerce was only responsible for 16% of total retail sales between offline and online. Online commerce is still like an adolescent, growing into adulthood. Offline commerce is, technically, still king although E-Commerce is growing year-after-year and is the future. By picking up this book, consuming it, and following through with the strategies being shared in this group that are following current trends, your business has the potential to either stay a market leader or become one.

However, just like any other book, this is information. This isn't implementation. The first step is reading through this book and you are taking it, congrats. However, action equals results therefore you must implement fast before your competition, old and new, beats you. With that said, grab a highlighter, post-its, an ipad with an apple pencil, or a notebook with a pencil, and be the best student that you can be as you consume this invaluable book. You are about to dive into strategies and tactics shared by some of the best Facebook Advertisers, literally on the planet, that I've had the great privilege to spend time with. Don't waste this opportunity because on the other side of this book could be incredible, exponential growth for your company if you take action.

Discover how the ARM5 Formula has helped companies
do $93,000 in one day (138,497% ROAS),
$330,000 during Black Friday 2019 (6349% ROAS),
$274,000 during Valentine's Day 2019 (1531% ROAS),
and an average 1480.61% ROAS throughout 2019 by
*going to **www.joshmarsden.com/success***

CHAPTER 2

Facebook and Instagram advertising are thriving! Here's how to win in 2020

The year 2020 is THE YEAR to drive incredible growth in your E-Commerce business by using Facebook and Instagram Advertising. For one, E-Commerce is growing. There are estimated to be $2.05 billion global digital buyers in 2020. More and more people are getting comfortable making purchases online. More and more businesses are also making the transition into an online storefront. Yet, in 2019, E-Commerce sales were only responsible for 16% of total retail sales. We are far from the peak of online E-Commerce with augmented and virtual reality coming in the future.

We are also far from the peak of Facebook advertising here in 2020. In 2019, the average price for ads decreased by 6% vs. 2018 signifying a continued decrease to advertise here in 2020. The level of activity on Facebook is growing too with the monthly active users on Facebook topping out at 2.4 billion in 2019. The user base is still growing. Only 69% of adults are on Facebook leaving 31% of adults still not! Everyone on Facebook accesses the app on average 8 times per day. Finally, 26% of users who clicked on ads went on to make purchases. Plus, Facebook advertising ranked #2 behind Google in 2019 for total digital advertising market share with $26 billion reported vs. Google's $46 billion reported. Bottom line is that Facebook hasn't peaked yet.

While Facebook as a social network is growing giving E-Commerce businesses and advertisers even more opportunity than what has already been on the network in the past, the question still comes down to whether you should focus attention or more of it on Facebook Advertising. Just because others are doing it, does not mean that you should do it too. It comes down to the following: by using Facebook advertising, can you acquire customers at a cost that yields profit? However, this question isn't just about Facebook advertising. It's also about the performance of your store and this is a massive oversight that many business owners make when running Facebook advertising or any digital advertising.

To explain this point further, here's an example. According to statistics, the average cost per click on Facebook is reported to be $1.72, with costs varying depending on the market that you are in or the audience that you are after. For example, the apparel industry averages a .45 cost per click. Let's say that you are targeting an older demographic with a clothing line. This raises the cost per click to $2.50 since there are fewer people 55+ on Facebook, making it a more competitive audience to go after and thereby raising the cost. According to more real statistics, the average E-Commerce store converts at about 2%. In one month, if you have a budget of $3000 and you are paying $2.50 per click, then that means that you were able to get 1200 visits to your store that month. At a 2% conversion rate, that means that you were able to get 24 customers. If you have an average order value, meaning the average total sale price when someone checks out in your store, of $155, you just made $3720 in revenue. That's not profit. If you have a 40% profit margin, then you actually made $1488 after spending $3000 in Facebook advertising. That's not a good result, yet, but it's a start.

Now, this example doesn't mean that you shouldn't advertise on Facebook if this scares you. It just means that you have opportunities to improve your conversion rates and average order value. The whole outcome changes if you can get your store to convert at double the conversion rate and you can raise your average order value to $200. These improvements yield double the customers at 48, $9,600 in revenue or, at the same 40% profit margin, $3,840 in profit. After the $3000 ad spend, that may not seem like much but acquiring customers at break-even, or better, is positive. You just added 24 customers to your customer base predictably without losing money. That's a win.

The key to reaping ROI from Facebook or Instagram advertising is what happens after you acquire a customer. As a business, you have to continue to add value with additional offers. This comes down to having an effective customer value journey strategy and process designed to monetize each customer fully. When you do this, you are focusing on the #1 metric of business, customer lifetime value. If you are maximizing the average customer lifetime value instead of just focusing on front-end customer acquisition, then you can see a bigger ROI for your ad spend. For example, if you have an effective customer value journey strategy and process that yields an average customer lifetime value of $600, then you made $28,800 in revenue, not just $9,600, off the reported 48 customers. With the 40% example profit margin, that's $11,520 off of $3000 in ad spend for a 384% ROI.

What this all means for you is that there's a big market that you can reach through advertising on Facebook and that market is growing. It also means that if you haven't taken advantage of Facebook advertising as a marketing channel for your business, you are missing considerable results and market share in your market. If you don't, someone else will and with 93% of social media marketers are reported to be using Facebook advertising, will they shall.

More importantly, this also means that to succeed with Facebook or Instagram advertising, you have to understand that it's about more than just running ads on Facebook or Instagram. Your store, your strategy, your follow-up, your product mix, and your process, all contribute to the effectiveness and profits of your Facebook or Instagram advertising usage. Real marketers win with Facebook and Instagram advertising because they understand this. You must become a real marketer that uses math and understands everything that it takes to be successful with Facebook and Instagram advertising. That's how to maximize its effectiveness in your business and to win with Facebook advertising in 2020.

CHAPTER 3

Josh Marsden: The Architect of the Powerful ARM5 Formula, a Strategy, Process and Philosophy for Maximizing Advertising ROI

As mentioned at the beginning of the book, I got my start as an Infusionsoft Certified Partner consulting with small businesses on how they could improve their use of Infusionsoft. This included helping companies generate more results from their email marketing automation or it meant helping them automate parts of their business, due to the well-rounded nature of Infusionsoft. Initially, I was a solopreneur, doing everything and I meant everything on my own. Early on, I didn't really know much about being an entrepreneur or business owner. I had some solid corporate management experience where I did very well for myself but that's a completely different arena. Luckily, most of my prior experience was in sales and sales is easily the #1 responsibility of a business owner. With this honed skill from over a decade of experience, I was able to get the business going and keep it going, even when I hit some rough patches.

In 2014, I knew that while I could help companies automate their businesses using Infusionsoft, my real passion was in helping companies' generate results. I attribute this back to the fact that I had always been in professional positions that were results-based. Getting results, whether it was for my own business or prior employers, gave me my thrills. This led me to focus on becoming the best direct-response and digital marketer that

I could be. I started reading books, listening to podcasts, reading blogs, and, eventually, this led to becoming a valuable member of a paid community called Digital Marketer Engage by Digital Marketer. Then, I ended up going to my first business event in late 2014 by the same company. At this event, Digital Marketer offered an opportunity for attendees to become Certified Partners with the company. A competitor of mine whom I had a rivalry with, who was also at the event, jumped on this right away and was the very first to sign up. Upon seeing this and being a fierce competitor myself, I had to do it even if it was $10,000, which was a lot at the time. This impulsive, yet calculated risk, led to some early, very impactful relationships with the leadership team at Digital Marketer in Richard Lindner, Ryan Deiss, and Roland Frasier.

After that, I decided to niche the company in Sales Funnels services in early 2015. If you don't know what Sales Funnels are, they are essentially a process that prospects go through to become a lead and a customer while maximizing transaction value. This process consists of web pages and marketing automation, the latter driving follow-up. With the Digital Marketer Certified Partner prestige, my prices went up to $10,000 - $25,000 per Sales Funnel project. Within the first 12 months of changing my business model, I had my first $75,000 sales month, so I definitely felt like I was on the right track.

Then, in early 2016, I decided to dive into learning digital advertising with Facebook and Google advertising. I did this through Digital Marketer's resources that I had access to, books, courses, and through my network. I added Facebook advertising services shortly thereafter as an additional service to sell. I also started expanding my network further by going to events by Baby Bathwater Institute, Todd Herman, David Gonzalez, Digital Marketer, and various others in the internet marketing community. I also joined my first Mastermind investing $25,000 for a year to learn from one of the best in online business in Ryan Levesque. This allowed me to also add in Ask Method services into my service offering mix.

Every year since 2013, my business has grown between 30% - 70%. We added omnichannel advertising services with experienced team members and processes in 2018 to adapt to the trend of how E-Commerce businesses should be using omnichannel advertising. Now, after over 18 months of testing, we have a tested, proven strategy and process, called the ARM5 Formula for helping 7-8 figure E-Commerce companies use digital advertising effectively, profitably, and at scale, wrapped into two service plans at $5000 or $10,000 per month with a performance bonus included. It's been a journey, that's for sure. There have been some tough times since 2013, absolutely. Overall though, I wouldn't change anything. I'm proud to have built a company, team, and culture in my company, CVO Acceleration, around generating results for our clients while providing professional, high-quality experiences.

FUNDAMENTAL DIFFERENCES BETWEEN FACEBOOK AND INSTAGRAM ADS

Facebook and Instagram advertising both have overlapping similarities. They both have user bases with the same intent, although Facebook as a company is working hard to change that. What I mean by this is that the main intent of people on both social networks is to consume content, interact with their friends, network, and stay on top of the news. Unlike Google, they are not on there to look for a solution to their problem and to potentially purchase a product or service. Therefore, advertising on both Facebook and Instagram requires disruptive marketing using attention-grabbing, relevant ads. Within the first 5 seconds, you have to give the prospect a reason to stop. Then the creative, on either advertising channel, have to give people reason to continue to watch, then to take action. That doesn't change between channels.

What is different though is the demographic. Instagram is heavily 35 and under. If you are trying to sell products to a demographic below the age of 35, then Instagram should definitely be in your marketing strategy. Facebook has a wider spectrum of demographics and, although it does have users under the age of 35, the younger demographic prefers to use Instagram over Facebook so you'll want to factor that into your strategy too.

Now, Instagram has shorter-form content while Facebook has longer-form content. This causes the advertising creatives to differ between the two advertising channels, sometimes to a large degree. With Instagram, for example, your videos on the feed can only be up to 60 seconds while on Facebook, there is no limitation here, although you shouldn't exceed 5 minutes in my opinion. When strategizing the creative direction of an advertisement, this plays a massive role in how we structure the video creative. You have to get to the hook, the message, the benefits, and the impact that you are trying to make with your video creative much faster in an Instagram video ad vs. a Facebook video ad. The nice thing here though is that if you can create a creative that works on Instagram, it's probably going to work very well on Facebook as well.

The use of messaging is also different between the two advertising channels. With Facebook, you can really use copywriting to persuade prospects to take action in your advertisement. As a direct-response copywriter myself, I love this benefit of Facebook advertising. With Instagram, although you can technically use copywriting in your ad, it's not quite as effective. For one, the users on Instagram have much shorter attention spans and are least likely to stop and read. Video and images drive the channel. Plus, Instagram ads have a limitation in that you can't have clickable links in a post on the news feed. When you are using direct-response copywriting in your ad and you are directing people to click a link that they can't click on, that really nullifies the whole idea of using long-form copywriting in an ad on Instagram. With that said, higher-ticket products, in our tests, convert higher on Facebook ads since we can actually use copywriting techniques to get conversions.

HOW THE ARM5 FORMULA WORKS

Although I call the ARM5 Formula a strategy and process, it's actually just as much a philosophy. The simple thought behind the ARM5 Formula is that in order to use digital advertising effectively, profitably, and be able to scale your advertising while maintaining profitable results, you have to focus on much more than just getting clicks from ads. You also have to focus on the conversion rates of the pages that you are driving people to, how you take someone from one purchase to several, how you follow-up with leads and customers to get them to buy or re-buy, and more. Yet, this all contributes to the ROI that you see from your advertising budget. That's why it's just as much of a philosophy as it is a strategy and process. If you are using digital advertising, which I firmly believe that every E-Commerce business owner should be doing, you have to have the right mindset that it's so much more than just getting targeted clicks from your ads.

The ARM5 Formula, as a strategy, comes down to a fundamental in marketing and that's using an effective prospect to customer journey. Since we are a Digital Marketer Certified Partner, we follow Digital Marketer's Customer Value Journey process for our clients. The ARM5 Formula pays respects to the Customer Value Journey in that it's designed to show the right ad to the right person at the right time. That's the strategic aspect of the ARM5 Formula. To break it down further, the first step of the strategy is using content, in the form of video or written content, to position a brand as an authority in the market that they are in. That's where the "A" in ARM comes from, authority. This also helps to acquire a person pixeled by the Facebook advertising pixel cheaper since it follows the trend that Facebook as a company wants advertisers to follow, showing appropriate content based on the Facebook user's relationship with the brand. They initiated this trend when they first rolled out relevance scores back in 2018 and have now evolved this singular score into 3 different scores, quality ranking, engagement rate, and conversion rate. In this case, this first step is generating awareness. The best part is that because of our effective retargeting and web page optimization, these awareness ads typically end up with a positive ROI.

Once we have that awareness, at a cheaper rate than just showing an offer to a cold audience, now we use retargeting to move people towards becoming a lead and a customer. Since the pixeled prospect saw value from the brand, they are much more receptive to offers and are much more willing to take steps to reciprocate that value. That's where the "R" comes from in ARM, standing for reciprocity. In our tests, offers convert much higher when they have an already established relationship with a brand, because of the effective use of content in a brand's marketing awareness stage. Also, costs to acquire customers are reduced, in most cases, following this approach.

We also have a specific segmented retargeting strategy in the ARM5 Formula for getting website visits, add to carts, and initiate checkouts to come back and finish their purchase in this stage of our process. We've had up to a 10,817 ROAS following our process here meaning that in this specific case, we are seeing $108 back for every $1 spent on these retargeting ads. The monetization doesn't end there either. In fact, this is only where it begins.

The biggest aspect of the ARM5 Formula is in the Monetization strategies incorporated into it. That's where the "M" comes in and the 5, for our 5 profit amplifiers authority, trust, monetization, testing matrix, and persuasion. Our monetization strategy is relatively simple in that it's all about the more offers that you make, the more money you make. Now, when I say this, it doesn't mean to be spammy. If you are continuing to serve valuable content to attract a cold audience and nurture your warmer audiences, then you are earning the right to make offers to your list and customers at a regular frequency of 7 pieces of content to 1 offer. Some examples of what we do as a part of monetization includes optimizing the upsell and downsell process to raise average order value by 200%+, creating a year-round promotional calendar and executing these promotions following our tested, proven promo funnel strategy that's made clients upwards of 5200% ROI from ads, and implementing monetization funnels offering profit maximizers aka high-ticket offers like bundles, multiple orders in one offer, etc. to customers to raise customer lifetime value by 200%+, just to name a few. Email, Facebook Messenger, and SMS automation are all part of our process too so we can maximize the return on advertising through automated follow-up marketing.

As far as the advertising side, we concentrate a lot of our efforts on using Facebook ads to acquire leads through Facebook lead ads or driving traffic to targeted lead magnet opt-in landing pages, which are typically downloadable guides, video training, or a quiz following Ryan Levesque's Ask Method process. Facebook's wide array of targeting capabilities, in my opinion, allows us to acquire the best possible prospects for companies that we work with. We also use Facebook dynamic product ads to retarget customers and get them to come back and buy. We also use Facebook retargeting ads to get customers to return to a store around the time when a consumable product is about to expire. We are able to do this by tagging customers in Klaviyo after they make their purchase of a consumable product and then putting them in a custom audience after 30 days have passed, for example. Omnichannel advertising works really well here too since Google advertising is a very effective monetization channel when combined with Facebook advertising.

Finally, Wicked Reports has been an absolute game-changer for us with the companies we work with. We require all clients to have Wicked Reports to work with us so we can measure ROI from each channel 100% accurately instead of relying on Facebook, for example, to give us this data. For example, Wicked Reports matches each click from Facebook ads with orders from Shopify instead of Facebook firing a pixel and attributing results to their ads that way. Wicked Reports even give us ROI data from each ad and audience so we know which ads or audiences are giving us the biggest results so we can quickly test scaling audiences or ads to bigger results. Finally, the attribution reporting in Wicked Reports also helps us identify which audiences or ads are leading to the most profitable opt-ins or customers so we can also quickly test scaling audiences or ads from these reports.

CURRENT TRENDS

There are 3 current trends that I see happening right now. For one, Facebook and Instagram advertising is getting more competitive and will continue to be competitive, even more so in the future. I don't see it as something to worry about but I do see it as a healthy challenge for E-Commerce businesses and marketers to adapt to. The best marketers and businesses will win, hands down. If you don't understand how to use marketing to turn prospects into leads and customers, you will lose. If you don't understand how to run a really good business with great metrics, in average order value and customer lifetime value, you will lose. I see that happening right now even with fewer cases of new entrepreneurs winning big early in their journeys. I've been in this industry for over 7 years so I've seen the early days of new entrepreneurs jumping online and generating ridiculous profits using Facebook ads all the way to the modern days of how it takes good business optimization with great marketing to win with Facebook ads.

Another trend that I see is Facebook becoming two things: a media conglomerate to replace television and an environment with more buying intent. I actually see YouTube and Facebook, right now, as the modern-day television with commercial ads in the form of YouTube or Facebook Video ads. You can literally reach millions of people, super-targeted, and cost-effectively right now and television advertising has never been this way. In regards to Facebook transforming from a social network to a multi-faceted consumer network, that's happening right now with the Marketplace for example. I see Facebook continuing to mold the behaviors of its users, as they have been, so that people are active on the network and they use it to handle transactions. We already have the ability to do transactions through Facebook messenger as it is.

Finally, I also see more and more people flocking to Instagram. Instagram is growing in popularity and shows no signs of slowing down. We also live in a society that's all about efficiency with short attention spans and Instagram is an efficient social network experience that will continue to appeal to more and more people that want their "social network fix" quickly. I think, eventually, Snapchat will die out and Instagram will take over too. Instagram will continue to grow alongside E-Commerce too since Instagram has built-in E-Commerce functionality with no signs of slowing down developments of new features to appeal to E-Commerce.

CHAPTER 4

Jason Hornung: The Best Direct-Response Marketer in Facebook Advertising

I got started as an entrepreneur when I was 23. I was recruited to be an insurance agency owner, and I started from scratch with no money or clients. What they teach you to do is go out and sell by knocking on peoples' doors. So for the first 2 years of that business, I spent 80 hours a week hustling. I forced myself to cold call 300 people a day and to walk into 15 different businesses a day to ask if I could quote their insurance. I started this business 2 months after my second daughter was born, and my third daughter was born during that time. The amount of time that I was working caused me to miss a lot of crucial time with them when they were younger and it caused a lot of constraints on my marriage. I was burned out. I hated having to feel like I was begging people just to allow me to quote their business, so I started asking myself what I needed to do. It boiled down to needing to get people contacting me.

As I was thinking about that, it became clear that I needed to figure out how to attract people to me. I started researching attraction marketing in 2005, and that's how I came across Dan Kennedy and bought his Ultimate Sales Letter book. I got on his newsletters and became convinced that learning direct response copy was going to be the key to me having financial freedom, and I started applying that to my insurance business. I started writing direct mail pieces and mailing them out, trying to get people to contact me for quotes on their insurance.

For the first few mailers, I had my oldest daughter in my office, helping me lick envelopes and put stamps on them. I hand wrote them all. I wrote this big letter that took me weeks to write along with numerous revisions. I spent over $1,000 on the list and postage, and I mailed all these letters out. Nothing came back. I'm not the kind of guy that gives up easily, so I did it again, and again, and again. And the first 4 times, it all flopped. But I stuck with it, and the fifth one worked!

I grew my insurance agency that way. I won all the company awards for all the lines of sales. They thought I was an all-star. But I became increasingly disenfranchised with the insurance business and a lot of the things that were going on in it. They tell you you're a business owner, but they don't treat you like one. They treat you like an employee and you have to act like an employee, but they call you a business owner for tax purposes. You get all the tax burden, and they can get rid of you at any time. I wanted to be in control to do my own thing.

I loved marketing, so I walked away from my book of business on December 1st of 2009, to go market online full-time. I didn't know what I was going to do. I was really deep in the Clickbank world at the time, so I was convinced I would be able to just sell somebody else's ebook and make millions of dollars doing that as an affiliate.

I started doing all of the affiliate stuff in 2010, and I'd get some things that worked and others that didn't. By the end of the year, I was dead broke. I had cashed out my retirement accounts and put 80 grand on credit cards, and it was December. I had no money left. I hadn't paid the mortgage, hadn't bought my kids any Christmas presents, and I had put the last $2,000 that I had on a credit card on a coaching package from James Frances. On a call with him, I got real and explained that I didn't know what to do and how everything had spiraled. He introduced me to the website Upwork, though it was called oDesk at the time.

It let me get in touch with people and businesses that needed my skills, so I created a profile and started applying for jobs. Within 3 days, I had a client wire transfer me $3,000 for 30 days worth of work. I got that money right before I needed to pay the mortgage before the grace period was over, and I had enough to buy the kids presents, too. I did a great job for that client and we made a lot of money together. They started telling other people about me, and before you know it, I have this agency where I'm doing all kinds of marketing for other clients.

By 2013 we were doing all kinds of things, like LinkedIn ads, email drops, SEO, building info products, you name it. In 2013, my clients were wondering about Facebook ads, and that's when I went into Facebook. Within 6 months, I became this Facebook guru.

FUNDAMENTAL DIFFERENCES BETWEEN FACEBOOK AND INSTAGRAM ADS

The base difference is that you have to be a lot punchier on Instagram. At most, you have 60 seconds for a video. For eCommerce, that's not really a big issue because most eCommerce people aren't doing long videos. You don't have to set a lot of things up, but you need to have the formatting right. We're seeing square formatting work the best across the board, but especially on Instagram.

EFFECTIVE STRATEGIES

One thing that I highly recommend to my eCommerce clients advertising on Instagram is that you make a version of your video that is formatted specifically for Stories: a 15-second version. A lot of people have a hard time believing a 15-second video can sell something, but with how short attention spans are, you can get a clear, concise message in 15 seconds and sell a lot of your product. That's where a lot of the best inventory is sitting right now, and that's where the best eyeballs are with the most dollars. So having that format and adjusting your creative to that placement is absolutely crucial to long-term success and scale for eCommerce right now.

Billy Mays passed away a few years ago, but he's still one of the best pitchmen ever. He sold billions of dollars worth of products on infomercials, and I came across a document that is a transcript from his 21 best infomercials. Every single one starts with a question, and that is what I teach my students: use a flagging question in your ads. This works really well on Instagram Stories. You want to ask a question that identifies your target audience, preferably in a format that implies some kind of pain your product solves. That's the best way to flag a customer with one sentence. For example, if you're selling a pet stain remover, your video should start with something like, "Are you sick and tired of these unsightly pet stains and smells in your carpet?"

But a lot of people in eCommerce get hung up on wondering how something like a t-shirt is going to fix someone's pain. But in those cases, it's not necessarily a pain you want to fix, but a "gain" that they're looking for. So it would be more along the lines of, "Are you looking for a super cool t-shirt of your favorite band?" You modify it to identify your ideal customer and get them to a place where they're ready to make a purchase from you. Next, you say, "Here's what I have for you. Swipe up to learn more." Tell them what you have and then give them a call to action to swipe up. It's simple.

You don't even go over the offer in the video. With eCommerce in particular, we do all of that on the product page. In these ads, we would actually use the conversions objective and drive people straight to the product page. This means you get very cost-effective clicks, with click-through rates being 5%-10% while cost per click is less than 25 cents.

On the Facebook side of things, if you're starting with a brand new product, a strategy we like to deploy is to find specific interests that have a high probability of containing the customer we're looking for. We'll run campaigns using Campaign Budget Optimization (CBO) where we put 1-3 of those audiences inside the campaign, and each one has its own ad set. We have one creative that goes out to those audiences, so we're testing the audiences plus the creative within the campaign budgets. We leave the $100 a day default on there. That's what we do for testing and we start to build the data from that. Once we start getting data, we move onto retargeting using Dynamic Product Ads and the catalog sales objective. Our default there is to start with just the 14-day add-to-cart audience, with a creative there that runs that. We don't offer any incentives for people to come back to buy, we just overcome objections that people have at that point. The cold traffic copy and the ads are all about the offer, and we just drive them to the product page and retarget them.

CURRENT TRENDS

Looking specifically within the eCommerce space, Facebook is really trying to push out dropshippers that have longer shipping times. Facebook has people doing account scoring and they are particular about scoring eCommerce companies. If you're a new eCommerce company, you get some leeway in the beginning, and this is where a lot of people are seeing things that used to work going downhill. Facebook starts getting data on who's buying from you and they start privately sending those people surveys, which determines your account score. You don't even know anything about this score until it gets low and you start getting emails telling you it's low and they'll shut your account down if you don't fix it.

Once your score gets low, Facebook starts charging you higher CPMs, so the cost of traffic goes up. They limit the quality of traffic so that you get lower-tier traffic at the same time, so it doesn't convert as well. A lot of it has nothing to do with the creative or the audience but instead has to do with the business model and how people are reporting their interactions to Facebook. If you continue to have issues, you could be on the verge of getting kicked off the platform, but if you can get to the point where you have fast shipping and you're building a solid brand that's focused on customer service, there shouldn't be any issues at all.

This leads to some thinking that Facebook hates dropshipping. They only hate dropshipping when you take 2 or 3 weeks to deliver the product to your customers because customers hate that and won't want to buy anything on Facebook anymore.

Another trend I'm seeing is that many eCommerce businesses we work with rely completely on one front-end product. They have no up-sells or down-sells, and they do little to no follow-up at all. Most of them will have, at best, a 7-part email sequence that follows up with people. But if you really want to make margins and have a long-term sustainable business, you have to be running promotions on a regular basis. You have to be communicating with your buyers frequently. You have to be cross-selling, down-selling, and up-selling. You have to call these people and operate as a legitimate business.

Considering all of this, eCommerce companies should stop putting out offers and ads that people don't like. That's a big thing in eCommerce. Most of the ads I see and creatives that people put together are all about the offer, and it's a pitch-fest without any story or build-up. People are starting to reject it. This is why the creative and having a tight brand story in your ads are both absolutely crucial. If you treat it like it's all about the price and the discount, people are going to get really skeptical.

Ad campaigns need to tell the right story and build the brand while moving people into the funnel to make an offer. One way that we have clients doing that is by using a full-funnel structure with the ad sequencing. We'll use top-of-the-funnel objectives, like page engagements and video views, and we'll put together a creative that tells the brand story. This can be hard for dropshippers, who don't usually have a reason beyond wanting to sell a hot product. That's part of why you shouldn't build a business solely for the purpose of how you think you're going to make money. It has to be something you actually believe in or you'll never be able to differentiate your product from anyone else's. You might be able to just mimic what other people are doing and hope it works for a while, without any of your own effort or thought. But everything Facebook, Instagram, and other ad platforms are doing is trying to prevent that sort of thing.

When it comes to Ad Account structure, we use page engagement or video views, with a 60-second video that explains why the product was created and what problem it solves, and we give them the ability to learn more by sending them to a page on the website to do their initial research. In a lot of these cases, people aren't even aware of the product or that they need it, so we have to begin that education there. Then we retarget people who watch a percentage of the video and people who have been to the landing pages. At this point, we use more direct-to-buy ads to send them straight to the product page. We'll only do this when we're trying to get more scale in the performance out of the campaign after we've proven the offer.

When we're starting completely from scratch, we're going to go straight to direct offer ads with a bit of a story element in the ad copy. We send that straight to the product page because we want to see if people want to buy that thing. A lot of people create these expanded funnels and spend money on these ads just to find proof of concept, but all that does is layer on extra expenses on testing a product with ads. You'll want to use these kinds of strategies when you go to scale sales once you have proof that the market will buy the offer.

WHAT'S TO COME

I think, as time passes, Facebook and Instagram are just going to keep tightening the belt. Everything that's been going on with Facebook recently is following everything Google did back in 2012 and 2013. Ad platforms first let marketers "blow it all up," and then businesses come in and kick the marketers out.

Succeeding with ads is all about getting more offers in the pipeline--especially bigger ticket, back-end offers that you can sell, cross-sell, or cross-promote--and making joint venture offers with other businesses if you can't come up with offers yourself that make sense. That's tough for eCommerce people; it's not like an information business where you can sell a back-end $5,000 coaching program. In the eCommerce space, it's all about developing joint ventures with other business partners who have products and services that relate to your offer, that you can promote on the back-end, along with developing your own additional products so you can keep rotating around other products to your existing customers. Getting that lifetime customer value higher is key to succeeding with ads.

According to the Brooks Institute, you have a 6% chance of doing business with somebody who's never done business with you before. Out of all of our best eCommerce stores, when we drive traffic from an ad straight to the product page, we'll get about a 6% conversion rate in the best scenario. Usually, it's 1%-3%, and there are a lot of people that were at 3% who have been knocked down. With a new business, you only have a 6% chance of doing business with someone, and everyone focuses their time and effort on that fresh blood.

However, you have a 50% chance of doing business with somebody who has already done business with you before. Most people don't spend a lick of money, time, or effort on selling to their already existing customer base, but that's where you should really focus most of your attention: getting more out of your existing customers instead of trying to get more customers. The cost of getting new customers on the front-end is only getting higher, which is why you have to have back-end systems in place at the same time to monetize your customer base.

Over the course of this year, most eCommerce companies have been seeing their conversion rates drop and their CPMs go up. That's the biggest complaint I get. In the newest algorithm change, Facebook placed a huge amount of importance on your page speed. They tie that directly to the user experience. If your page speed loading time is 6 seconds or more, your conversion rate will never be more than 1.5% on your eCommerce store. If you can get it down to 3 seconds or less, it will go up to 3% or more automatically, without changing anything else. And the ad networks, when your page loads faster, charge you a lower CPM and Facebook gives you higher ad diagnostic scores. Trying to speed up load times is what we're doing with all of our high-volume eCommerce companies right now, without changing anything else. We're able to triple the conversion rate and thus get ROIs to where they need to be.

MORE EFFECTIVE STRATEGIES!

Few people actually target the fans on their fan page. It seems like a no brainer to do this. What I've been doing is running campaigns to increase my fans. I have a $29.95 low-ticket eCommerce product that I run ads to with my page fans as the target audience, and I'm getting nearly a 3:1 return when I count the ad spend total. I don't see anybody else using that model.

There's another strategy I call rapid scale, and what we're doing is testing an offer to a broad market. We start with a campaign using CBO with $100 a day as the budget and leave it at the lowest cost bid setting. In the ad set, we put no targeting, so there's no specific interest. There's no lookalike or custom audience. All we're doing is setting the demographics for our audience, such as women 30-55 in the US. We exclude anybody who's already bought, and we optimize for the purchase action. We use the purchase conversion objective and we put a 1-day click window on there for the optimization window. We put 1 ad in the ad set and it's an image of the product. Then we have the copy in there and we're going to drive the traffic straight to the product page. The next day we look at the numbers. If we have sales and they're within our key performance indicators (KPI), we're going to leave it on. If not, we shut it off. If it has sales but it's outside of KPI, we may or may not leave it on depending on how far out of KPI it is. If it's more than twice our KPI, we turn it off. If it's only about 50% more than our KPI, we leave it on because the algorithm can continue to optimize and it can get better over time.

If it's at least half of our KPIs, we're going to rapid-scale that ad set. We increase the daily budget from $100 to $1,000 immediately, and we put a rule on that campaign that if it has spent more than 2-4 times our KPIs, we turn it off. But in most cases, that isn't necessary. So we've instantly gone from $100 to $1,000 a day and we have the biggest, broadest audience we could possibly have. We can continue to incrementally scale that budget and we're able to take them up to $4,000 per day within a week while maintaining KPIs. Of course, that all only works if the offer is good and if it has a bigger, broader market fit.

Part of the way the algorithm works is that it needs a lot of conversions. In order to optimize properly, it wants 50-100 conversions a day. For example, let's say in a scenario where we have a $20 CPA, a $1,000 daily budget will allow us to get 50 conversions a day. For whatever reason, the budget signals to the algorithm that you're a serious player because it can get the conversions needed, and it optimizes better for you.

*Discover how the ARM5 Formula has helped companies do $93,000 in one day (138,497% ROAS), $330,000 during Black Friday 2019 (6349% ROAS), $274,000 during Valentine's Day 2019 (1531% ROAS), and an average 1480.61% ROAS throughout 2019 by going to **www.joshmarsden.com/success***

CHAPTER 5

Jeremy Howie: Mark Zuckerberg's Personally Trusted Facebook Advertiser

I work in my company Enlightened Marketing while also being a single father, raising my 7-year-old son. I'm also on Facebook's Small Business Council where I've met with Mark Zuckerberg and toured Facebook HQ on multiple occasions. I've been taking a step back from the agency, working more on the consultancy side in the Facebook marketing world, which is working out nicely. I'm getting a lot of profit share and equity deals, instead of scaling agency clients.

My passion is marketing and Facebook, but I also am dating and playing guitar. I think it's really good for a marketer's brain. It gets the right parts of the brain firing and gets that creativity going. I actually see it come out in my Facebook marketing. Even dating can be applied to marketing. If you think of the online dating sites, there's not a lot of integrity on these sites. If you think of ghosting--someone just disappears after you start talking to them--you wouldn't do that to someone on the street when you're on the sidewalk talking to them. So I think that can be applied to marketing: market like you would converse with someone face-to-face. It's a good learning experience, and it shines a lot of light on things within us.

FUNDAMENTAL DIFFERENCES BETWEEN FACEBOOK AND INSTAGRAM ADS

I think it's the experience as a whole. You have the typical things people think about, like the age demographic, but that isn't always true. Even so, you tend to have a younger demographic on Instagram. The experience is faster on Instagram, although both are super fast now. It's more about the moment and the experience on Instagram. But honestly, I don't go into a lot of that, unless we're getting into designing a specific image, video, or Stories ad. I let the data do the speaking. I or my design team will make images at times that are 1080 by 1080, optimized for both Facebook and Instagram. From there, I let the conversion algorithm do the speaking.

What's interesting is that we hear all about the younger age demographic on Instagram. But as a marketer, you always want to test. I think many advertisers get complacent in that. As an example of the value of testing, I have a tax attorney partner that I've run years of ads for. Things like opt-ins to an ebook for resolving taxes are crushing it on Instagram, and it's about double the CPA on Facebook. And then, there are certain eCommerce niches where Instagram is getting the purchase conversions all day long, about a third of what Facebook is. Even still, there are other niches where Facebook is crushing it and Instagram isn't even getting clicked. So you always need to test what you're doing.

Even if you think you know what's going on, you need to test it. At times, I swear I see a pattern, but then I try to duplicate a Dynamic Creative ad for example, and I can't replicate its performance. It can be completely random. I'll be in dropshipping one day, an established brand another, and then lead gen after that. I think the reason why duplicating success is challenging is because of platform saturation. Facebook Mobile is completely saturated now, and Instagram still has some room for more media-buying. I think that has a lot to do with it.

Still, I'm always looking for patterns, since whatever is consistently performing is valuable.

On the Facebook side of things, a lot of what's working for me is what's been naturally evolving with Facebook. I mentioned Dynamic Creative, which is basically the ability to import multiple creatives, headlines, or copy in a single ad or ad set, and let Facebook decide what's working in what placement.

What I'll do, depending on the niche and what I'm after, is put in 4 or so different versions of 1080 by 1080 images into a slideshow. First, I'll create it as a 5- to 15-second video to make sure we have in-stream video covered. I'll also create it as a 30- to 60-second video. Sometimes I'll even let the client speak as long as they want because I'll never discount the potential value of a long video. We see the trends that videos are getting shorter, but I have friends in other niches who are getting $4, 60-minute in-feed video views. Never discount that aspect of it. I'll take the targeting in these ad sets and duplicate them into retargeting.

So often, I'll see a lot of different behavior in the retargeting side of things. I'll generally change 1-day click to 7-day click or 1-day view when I'm retargeting, because I'm looking at longer-term data that need more data to convert. Dynamic Creative is working really well for this. Facebook designed the Dynamic Creative as a testing platform, and it's out-converting Post IDs in most cases. When I use it on a new client, I'll set it up and let it run for a while to buy 30 days' worth of data and get some conversions, then go back and look at the reports. I'll ask myself, "What headline? What image? What description? What call-to-action? What's actually converting in each of the ad sets?" I'll pull that over into Post IDs, and we'll begin to scale.

I generally create customized reports on Facebook. The main KPIs I'll look for are advertising spend, reach, CPMs, link clicks, cost per link click, landing page views, and cost per landing page view. If it's eCommerce, I'll take it from Add to Cart, Initiate Checkout, and Purchase. If it's for lead gen, I'll take it from Lead to Submit Application, and check the cost per each of those standard events. I'll look at the full 30 days, especially the last 3 or 4 days, to see where it's trending as it's really stabilized.

In the drop-downs of the reports, I'll look at the Dynamic Creative reports. It will tell you that you can break it down by ad set or ad, though it's more like breaking it down by headline, image, video, and so on. I'll check all of the KPIs I listed. It's hard to teach that process because there are so many things in it, but you can see what's getting the best click-through rate. You can see what's getting the lowest cost per click. You can put that cost per click into an equation to figure out that you need X number of clicks to get X number of conversions. Eventually, you learn which images, headlines, etc. are crushing it in which category.

What's generally working in a Campaign Budget Optimization structure for me is that I've gone all the way from 2 ad sets all the way up to 40 or 50 and had success either way. If someone is trying to learn this or scale it, I would recommend starting with 5 ad sets. I'll start out with Dynamic Creative and those 5 ad sets, and I'll do one with my best interests. If I'm going for lookalikes, I'll say 1% lookalike leads, because I know that will start to take over once we get enough data for that lookalike to populate. I'll also do retargeting. If the customer has a buyer's list or a lead list, I'll upload that. Then, I'll test a wide-open audience and let Facebook optimize that. When I get a winner out of those, I'll do 5 ad sets of that winner. Then I'll use that winner and pull in the Post IDs of the top-performing images. It's a quick way to scale.

If you're a little more advanced and want to scale, what works well is starting off with that process, getting those Post IDs, and establishing a super ad that has thousands of comments and shares. If you're spending $500 or $1,000 a day or more, open it wide to the algorithm. Target everyone. You'll find out who the buyer is, and then you can scale pretty quickly from $1,000 a day to $10,000 a day.

On the Instagram side, everything depends on testing. I might plan for a short video, but as soon as I say that, images come in and they crush it. That's why I rarely ever do Instagram only. Even if it wins in a CBO Dynamic Creative test, I still leave it open, because that's where Facebook is going, leaving it more and more open. Obviously, 1080 by 1080 images and short videos work pretty well, though you can't go over 1 minute on Instagram.

If you wanted to test Instagram separately, I would say use 3 versions of images, a short slideshow video, and maybe a 30-second video and a 60-second video. But, whether it's Facebook or Instagram, you have to make sure you have that hook right in the first line. On Instagram, in the Instagram feed, only that first sentence is going to appear.

One thing that would work really well on Instagram is to create a source audience of Instagram page engagers--someone who saved a post on Instagram--and then create a lookalike around that. Target those people only on Instagram, with Instagram-optimized ads.

CURRENT TRENDS

As soon as I think I see a big trend, I see an instance where it's not the case. But overall on Facebook and Instagram, there's a widening up of targeting, providing more things for Facebook to optimize for. I've had people ask if, with Dynamic Creative and Campaign Budget Optimization, our jobs as Facebook marketers are going to go away. The answer is 2 parts.

Yes, Facebook is trying to make it ridiculously simple for a business owner to spend money. Not just in a post-boosting environment but in an actual data environment where Facebook can help people spend money and actually get results.

To answer the question of our jobs going away, no, because you can't replace 10 years of marketing knowledge. You can't replace strategy and you can't teach creative or funnels.

You can take the trends and their evolutions to a whole new level, too. Facebook, recently, is very into VR, and one of my goals as a marketer has been to become an expert in how to place ads in a VR environment. Even thinking just 5 years down the road, it gets pretty esoteric and mystical, but it's heading that way and it's just going to keep moving faster and faster. But it's exciting, as a marketer, figuring out how we continue to provide the user experience in an ads funnel atmosphere in VR and in whatever other directions it takes.

One of the most important things is to be involved with that evolution. No matter how much you want to be brick and mortar, you can no longer ignore that you have to go online. I'm in talks with a Middle Eastern perfume company. They have 21 regional locations and are looking to transform online. How do they do that? How do they expand into Saudi Arabia? You have to be connected.

Facebook's new mission is to bring the world closer together. You have to get connected. You have to be involved in groups and rely on experts. I still hire experts and coaches for things I don't know, even on Facebook.

Along with getting connected, branding yourself and your business is becoming more important. You can't be faceless as easily anymore. You have to have a strong brand and be authentic in your messaging. You need attraction marketing to provide value and a good user experience, and you need to deliver on what they pay you for.

It's important to stay involved in this evolution into Facebook Live, video, AI, VR, and beyond. Not just marketers, but businesses that capitalize on these things and do it well are going to stay apart from the competition.

EFFECTIVE STRATEGIES

I'm not a master of systems and processes and standard operating procedures. I'm very customized. For example, I haven't scaled an agency because I get too involved in the minutiae. One thing I'm finding I can scale, though, is event response ads on Facebook with live events. It works really well for brick and mortar, but there are ways to adapt it to digital. I've done a lot of it recently: musicians, concerts, dermatology, just about any business. About 90% of businesses would benefit from having butts in seats, whether it's a virtual butt or a literal one. You don't need a website; you can run a pixel based on people who respond to the event as interested, going, or interested in going. You can create engagement with the event, such as purchasing tickets from Eventbrite that you can send to people in Facebook Messenger after connecting ManyChat to these event response ads.

You can continue to stay in touch with them, and when you get into Facebook Live's webinar-type format, you can still use these event ads to promote your Facebook Live. Over time, you'll have 10 or 20 events and add them as the source audience to create a lookalike of going, of interested, or of purchased tickets.

You have this setup where you have an event-based ad, you have a few different images and a couple different videos, and you run your 5 ad sets. You run your interests and you run your lookalikes of purchased tickets or lookalikes of marked as going. You go wide open in another ad set with lookalikes of past attendees and another with lookalikes of buyers. You can never replicate butts in seats at events. You can never get better marketing than someone sitting in front of you (literally or metaphorically), learning from you, walking with you.

There's also a helpful loophole on event-based ads. You can get past the 20% text rule or the text overlay. I've used 75% or 80% text on event image-based ads. They don't get hit, penalized, or warned. That's when you can have the text in the image of the event itself.

Soon, Facebook will be opening up something called the Boost by Facebook Leaders Network. It's going to open up to a wider range. If you have a business or you're creating one or planning to create one, get involved with this. There will be selection criteria, but it's going to be more widely available than programs that they have opened up in the past. You'll have access to direct support, new products, and new ad tests. It's going to be a network, and it loops right back to what I said about getting connected. You'll have special privileges within Facebook, and it will hopefully be public. If you get involved with it, you'll get involved with other serious business owners and it will give you access to various special tools and, most importantly, data.

CHAPTER 6

Rory Stern: One of the Original Facebook Ads 'Guys'

I'm a Facebook ads guy. I hate to say that term because everybody's a Facebook ads guy these days, but I've been running Facebook ad traffic for 6 years. I've had my own agency for 3. We love running ads, figuring out offers, and tinkering with making things scalable.

FUNDAMENTAL DIFFERENCES BETWEEN FACEBOOK AND INSTAGRAM

I think it's how people use the platform. How are they interacting? What are they there for? I always say that Facebook is sort of an escape from reality. The average user is generally there to check in with friends and family, share cat memes and dog pictures, and just exist and try to find some kind of happiness for a few minutes. They're not looking for stuff to buy, although the great thing is that we can put the right offer in front of them and transform them into buyers.

Now, Instagram is not a platform I fully understand as in-depth as I do Facebook, but more or less it's an extension of Facebook ads. We see good results over there, but I'm not their demographic. I'm not really there to post pictures, scroll through, and post other pictures.

I think one of the main differences is that Instagram is really just pictures and video. The platform is all about super fast interaction. If I look at the major social networks, Facebook is more of a home base; there are lots of different things to do. There are pages, there are groups, there's the market place, there's just so much happening on Facebook. On Instagram, the way it is now, you're scrolling through a news feed looking at pictures, dropping a heart, maybe dropping a comment, and that's it. It's super bite-sized pieces of your day.

A lot has certainly changed, on the Facebook side of things. Last year, we were really seeing great results just doing more manual stuff and working the algorithm. We always ran the bulk of our ads to news feeds, and we used to run it to desktop and mobile with an expectation that mobile would get 80% of the traffic. In the last year, Instagram became a really big front runner for conversions and seeing great results. There are still instances where we work on desktop and mobile news feeds with ad campaigns and see great results, but we're launching almost all of our campaigns now with automatic placement. Facebook seems to be doing a really good job overall for serving up our ads to the right audience in the right place and getting conversions where we want them. But even a year ago, when Facebook was preaching about auto-placement, you could see that it wasn't dialed in just yet. You'd see a lot of your ad spend in certain accounts get pushed to the audience network, and it just didn't work. Back then, it was hard to trust auto-placement. But now, the setting seems to be doing a much better job. I'd say what's working now is 100% using the auto-placement setting. Today, with the advances in the algorithm, I have a lot more faith in it doing its job to get results with auto-placement on.

As for our mainstays, we still launch almost all of our campaigns with static images, though I do love getting video into the mix, especially with a demonstrable product. This is especially true for eCommerce companies, if you have a great product that you can show being used. Those ads are typically great winners. Of course, there have been some shifts in trends for what's been working. We used to pop on an ad in a lot of instances and feel really confident with our results in 24-36 hours. Now, we are absolutely seeing that it takes up to 72 hours. You have to give Facebook ads time to optimize. Facebook is definitely catching up to other more mature ad networks, but it takes time to get out of that sandbox of testing as an ad network to really get advertisers the best results.

Once you learn how to work the Facebook ads software, it's pretty easy. Now, Facebook ads themselves are not easy. Getting the ads to actually work and be profitable takes a lot of effort, commitment, and dedication. Differentiating autonomy, autonomous, automatic placement, bot work, and all that jargon doesn't make things any easier. If you don't understand how an algorithm works and what data you need to feed it and how, you're not going to get it.

A couple of years ago, one of the two leading 3rd party Facebook ad management campaign platforms that integrates with Facebook ads would boast about having a "set and forget" model, and how you could scale your campaigns at the push of a button. That never has been the case, and it's certainly not the case right now.

Facebook ads are harder than they've ever been. Part of that is the maturity of the platform and its advertisers. Part of that is that costs are going up due to higher competition, higher bids, and Facebook charging more. So many people have been indoctrinated into this mindset of putting $1 in, get $2 out, get $3 out, get $4 out, get $5 out. Three years ago, that was possible. Two years ago, you could still do it, but it was harder. You can still do it today, but it's not easy.

To be successful today, it takes a lot of strategy and thinking, though it's roughly the same amount of pushing buttons and making selections on optimization as 4 years ago. Four years ago, you could put an ad up and scale it from $100 a day to $2,000 a day, and it could theoretically run well for 6-12 months with daily optimization. But now, it seems like you're burning through ad creatives, copy, graphics, images, and video so much faster. You've got to watch things so much more carefully. The algorithm is fragile and the slightest tweak to anything that doesn't work throws everything else out of alignment faster than ever before.

We're working with an eCommerce client right now, with target CPAs of $35 or less and we're getting a ROAS of 200% or more. We've been doing a good job for this client, but their ad account was disabled on a Saturday night out of left field. We've never had a disapproved ad, so there have been no signs of any issues. We fought it, and after 5 appeals and working with our representative, we finally got the account back. But those $35 CPAs are now more like $55 or $65. So what happened? Something must've changed. Something threw off their algorithm. Now, after 2 weeks, we're starting to see the CPA come down and settle more, but that requires a lot of patience, confidence, and work. You have to constantly adapt.

Even if your offer worked 1 or 2 years ago, that doesn't mean it will always work. Every offer has a life cycle and a lot of people don't want to hear more about it. You have to provide value, rather than just sitting there saying how wonderful you or your product is. Nobody cares about that. Nobody cares who I am, what I've spent, what my experience is, or what clients I've had! What they care about are the answers to the questions that they're asking about Facebook ads. What makes something hard? How do you make it easier? How do you get it to work? You've got to look at where the biggest problem that you can fix is with your product. If you're truly an expert in your product and if your ad buyer is a true marketing expert, they're going to be able to break that down for you and help you out, and that's what it requires more than ever today to be effective with Facebook ads.

On the Instagram side of things, it's less clear for me. We see results on Instagram, but my focus is on Facebook. It's a lot harder now with auto-placement. You need to select ad sizes that are unique to those placements because Instagram stories are tall and thin. For the Instagram news feed, for example, it's a square. That's a lot different than our typical ad on Facebook, which is still the original 1200 by 628 pixels. Facebook is trying to push people to do more 1200 by 1200 or basically a 1:1 ratio. I think the key is making sure that your images or videos are optimized for that size so you get as many placements as possible. If it's not, your ad just looks horrible on Instagram. You have to test to figure out what works. You might be surprised. Plus, you might not be happy with what works because of the change in workflow required.

In a broader sense, it's definitely images that really stand out. Facebook is very heavy on imagery when it comes to stopping the scroll and capturing attention. Most Instagram ads are all images with very little copy. Instagram Stories are the same type of thing. You get 15-30 seconds, so you don't have a lot of time to make an impression. This means that really good images or short, punchy videos work great. Facebook tells my company directly what their best practices are and what their recommendations are across brand advertising, direct response advertising, and 15-second videos.

When it comes to what to do and what not to do, I think a lot of people are so consumed with the ROAS that they forget that a lot of advertising is really about how much they can pay to acquire a customer. The money is made on the back end, during the follow-up and the customer lifecycle. Stop worrying so much about your immediate ROAS and look at what a customer is worth to you. If you're spending $25 to acquire a customer on a $35 info-product, that's a $10 margin. If that's not enough for you because you don't have upsells that work, you don't have a coaching program, you don't have more products, or you can't provide more value, that's your biggest problem with your ads. You don't have a real business. Instead, you actually have an offer that is starting to not work.

WHAT THE FUTURE HOLDS

In the future, Facebook advertising is only going to continue to get more expensive. We're going to have a significantly harder time engineering profits. I think it is going to continue getting harder to constantly and regularly construct profitable campaigns on a regular basis for the majority of advertisers out there. However, there will be people who can still do it. It is only going to get more strict, though. With that said, compliance is everything.

Facebook is going wild right now with compliance. More and more people are talking about compliance, but most of them have got it all wrong.

We've had conversations directly with the compliance and policy team at Facebook. I was on the phone with one of the leaders of the business integrity department to say I was sick and tired of the inconsistency of policy enforcement, and of the inconsistency with the information we get back from Facebook support. I'm talking about front-line support, chat support, appeals, anything like that. Some of the higher level reps that you can get are good and I'm really fortunate to have one of those good ones but most advertisers don't get access to them. You get very basic, generic feedback, despite it being a billion dollar company making all of its revenue off of advertisers. Facebook needs to serve us. However, simultaneously, they don't have to serve us. That's their business model. They're getting money from us. They don't have to give us anything in return beyond ads.

The other part of this that's important is that Facebook isn't really changing their ad policy. They're just changing or switching emphasis on what they're actively enforcing more than they were before. With that said, policy and compliance are huge now.

I know one other trend that I'm hearing about in the community is that pixels are going to become less useful because of what certain browsers and companies are doing to block pixels.

What I'm hearing is that it's going to rely a lot more on behavioral targeting and behavioral activity than it will on interest targeting. At the end of the day, the pixel will always be there. It just may not be as effective in getting us results automatically in the future. Is the pixel there? Does it fire? Can we track it? Those are my concerns. Though tracking in general has really become horrible. Facebook has been notorious for over-reporting and having issues with their tracking. It seems this year it's become even worse. We've had clients using 3 different types of tracking software, and every single one of them has reported different numbers that didn't match up with their CRM that's tracking sales.

Regardless of any pixel changes, you should always pull your advertising spend out of Facebook, because that's not going to change. Pull your adspend out of Facebook, and your leads and sales numbers from your

CRM. You need to be able to match that up in your CRM. If you can't do that, that spells trouble because you can't reliably scale. In the future, you need to be on multiple advertising platforms. If you can't go into your CRM or a reporting tool and know where sales and revenue are coming from down to an ad creative or an audience, you're in trouble and you're going to be even more trouble going forward.

(This is why you need to read the bonus chapter at the end with Scott Desgrosseilliers of Wicked Reports.)

But how do you do that? It's simple. Pull your ad spend out of Facebook. It's also really good to be using Google Analytics with enhanced eCommerce tracking. It's great to use Google Analytics for mapping the customer journey. We have put heat maps on every single client's page now, every funnel, every website. We're looking at heat maps of landing pages. We build funnels to see where the drop-offs are. We record all website visitors to figure out what's going on behaviourally. If you don't know where your numbers are and if you don't have true data integrity, you're in trouble. Get that squared away now before you start to scale.

EFFECTIVE STRATEGIES

For us, it's just adaptability. We are looking at all the points in our funnels and campaigns and constantly asking, "Where can we optimize? Where can we increase conversions? Where can we provide more value? How can we increase the average order value? How can we increase the customer lifetime value?" You've got to be focused on those to be effective with Facebook ads, especially before you scale.

There are 2 trends and 2 approaches to ad buying. You can focus on lowering your ad cost or improving your average order value (AOV) and customer lifetime value (CLTV). Keep in mind, though, that you have more control over the AOV and CLTV.

You can't control ad costs, and ad costs are going to continue to go up. This means that if you're constantly trying to get your CPA down to as cheap as it possibly can be, you're going to get priced out of Facebook. We try to keep CPAs low, but what we really want is to get that AOV and CLTV higher. That is a big strategy that we work on with our clients. The strategy is to figure out how to increase your AOV. Then, figure out how to increase your customer lifetime value. The most basic strategy that is working right now with optimization is to look at your actual funnel or website where you are driving traffic, find out where the weak point is, and start testing copy, images, videos, structure changes, and more to get better ads performance.

Ad strategy is one component. If you're only focused on ad strategy, you might think this doesn't apply and you might ultimately get priced out of running ads. The first funnel that a typical business uses to get customers, which typically includes your lead magnet, your immediate sale, your upsell 1, and your upsell 2, is all front end acquisition. This is why you have to have upsells in place to help offset the advertising costs by bringing up the AOV of that first transition into becoming a customer.

So how do you bring up the AOV? You have to establish what your baseline metrics are. If you've got an offer and funnel that is converting at 4%, and they also buy upsell 1 at 10%, upsell 2 at 15%, and upsell 3 at 7%, you have to start asking what the problem is if you are still not profitable or able to scale with your ads driving traffic to your funnel or website.

First, what are the conversions and the pricing of your offers? We have to get our baseline numbers to identify what we can afford to pay to acquire a customer profitably or break even on the first transaction. Then you have to figure out what you're going to test to be able to achieve your baselines. You should focus on testing one variable at a time. We're not going to try and increase the sales conversion rate while also trying to increase the upsell 1 conversion rate. Pick 1 thing and focus on it. Write down your baseline numbers and start doing math. You can use Google Sheets, Microsoft Excel, or even tools like Geru. With a first upsell, I know from experience that the conversion rate could be realistically at 20%. I then ask myself, "What's it going to take to get it to 20%?" Do I need to test the headline? Do I need to test the price? If I choose price, I then form a hypothesis: if I lower the price, then that will increase conversions. Then, I consider this: with getting more upsell 1 conversions, will that help offset and/or ultimately raise the AOV? Because in this scenario I said upsell 1 is converting at 10%. Upsell 2 is at 15%. Perhaps then I consider sliding upsell 2 into the upsell 1 position because of the difference in conversion rates. That gives you an idea of how to think through optimizing your funnel or website when you are using Facebook ads to drive traffic to it.

*Discover how the ARM5 Formula has helped companies do $93,000 in one day (138,497% ROAS), $330,000 during Black Friday 2019 (6349% ROAS), $274,000 during Valentine's Day 2019 (1531% ROAS), and an average 1480.61% ROAS throughout 2019 by going to **www.joshmarsden.com/success***

CHAPTER 7

Jeremy Wainwright: 13-Year Digital Advertising Veteran and Dr. Axe's Secret Weapon

I work in Facebook and Instagram advertising exclusively in health spaces, with a lot of well-known supplement companies. Over the last year or so, I've stepped away from running an agency to run a host of my own products. I still consult from time to time and, like many other people, I still utilize Facebook and Instagram.

In the late 2000s, while searching the Internet, I realized that there had to be a way to make money on it. So I bought a $50 guide on how to make money online; it was less than half a dozen pages and told me that I needed to set up a content website with Google Adsense. Following the guide, I did, and by 3 weeks later I realized that nothing was going to happen and I wasn't going to make any money. But then I realized that the man I bought the $50 guide from managed to make money, so there had to be a way.

That led me down the interesting hole of affiliate marketing, and for 7 or 8 years I was an affiliate with mobile billing, app installs, and physical products, like skincare. I've been involved with web traffic on every place on the Internet you can think of at some time or another, and it led to me running into companies with strong brands that, nevertheless, didn't know how to sell products from an advertising standpoint. They would ask me, "Jeremy, do you know how to sell this?" and I would tell them, "I've been selling that for years."

For a period of time, for anyone trying to sell anything on the Internet, it was almost a requirement to have a link back to some sort of celebrity. Whether it was true or not, people were claiming their supplements and products have been featured by Dr. Oz and Oprah, for example. When it turned out that one of the companies I worked for, Dr. Axe, had actually been on Dr. Oz and Oprah, it was an amazing marriage. I was in the right place at the right time for a brand that eventually exploded. Now, they pull in 9 figures per year.

I have consulted for a number of other companies, but at the end of the day, it's a small space. Eventually, I did some dropshipping and sold some physical products, anywhere from $10-$1,000. Eventually, I realized that the key to making a business work is recurring revenue, generally with consumable products.

WHAT IS CBO?

It stands for Campaign Budget Optimization. Originally, you would put a whole host of ads into an ad set and then manage the budget. Facebook is supposed to be rolling out CBO in the near future, which will move the budget from the ad set to the campaign set. You will no longer be able to set budgets at the ad set level, and this will effectively give Facebook the ability to juggle those budgets between ad sets. If you still want control, you'll have to run just 1 ad set per campaign, which a lot of people do.

From a Facebook standpoint, CBO is just how someone runs their ads. As they move on through Facebook, it's going to become more and more important to make sure that however they are managing their budget via AdSense or CBO on a campaign level, each of those ad spend methods has a different angle. Facebook really only gives 3 different options.

Most people like testing 1 attribute at a time--offering a 10% discount, a 12% discount, and a 15% discount, which doesn't differentiate enough to make a difference--but my clients and I prefer testing 3 big, different things. Maybe the reason people aren't checking out is because it's expensive, so one of the ads will have a discount. The next ad will say free shipping. The next will offer some sort of trial.

FUNDAMENTAL DIFFERENCES BETWEEN FACEBOOK AND INSTAGRAM ADS

The biggest thing to keep in mind when tailoring an ad for Facebook or Instagram is demographics. Looking at Facebook, everyone knows the stereotype of its user base being full of mothers, grandmothers, and aunts. If a product skews towards the demographic of women over 45 and there are advertisements on both Facebook and Instagram, most of the results are going to be from Facebook because that's where the intended demographic is. Generally, Instagram is a little bit younger. The video needs to be a little bit shorter and punchier as, generally speaking, younger demographics have shorter attention spans and an ad needs to get to the point very quickly.

Listen to a podcast or read an article, and most of them will say the same thing: Facebook is getting more expensive, and advertisers should look elsewhere. But as far as I'm concerned, Facebook is great at what it does. It offers a ton of information about the users.

Most of my efficiency comes from 2 things. First of all, I make sure I'm targeting ads at the right places and keeping track of what results in a purchase and what doesn't.

The problem everyone else is running into is that they don't tailor their creatives, which is where the rest of my efficiency comes from. I just have to put in slightly more work than competitors do, so my creative is truly talking to the intended customer. The older method involved targeting a 30-year age range and then trying to use the exact same creative for that same 30 years, for both men and women. But now, the people who are doing slightly more work are the ones who are winning. It isn't a matter of hiring this specific copywriter and getting locked in a room. If a brand is already selling products, there are already people who have bought that product and would love to explain why.

Another thing I see successful clients doing is dedicating a lot of time to customer service. For businesses that don't do that, finding their marketing hooks and angles for use in ads is mostly a matter of sticking a bunch of marketing people in a room and thinking them up. When you compare that to getting feedback from real customers, this makes no sense and is a waste of time. The better creative strategy is to find customers, ask for their opinions, and use those in the ads.

When it comes to the Instagram side of things, it's been a really interesting place recently because organic reach--the unpaid distribution of an ad--is down. With less organic reach, advertisers have to pay for reach, instead. They put out tons of videos so that people watch them on Instagram, and those get steadily cheaper because they're just more inventory to keep track of and because distribution isn't free anymore.

As long as the video succeeds at soft-selling the product, it's doing its job. I'll use one of my clients in the sleep niche as an example. All of the videos for this client are all of the ways that you can naturally get better sleep: turn off the computer 2 hours before bed, put on blue blockers, don't eat terribly, exercise, etc. Everyone that is engaging with that content-- around 95% of views--is very engaged in trying to get better sleep. So, we have this audience of people in the demographic that we want to buy this product. On the whole, it's doing great.

As for tips and tricks, the big thing for a while was Instagram Stories. People were getting great results with Instagram Stories, and the "selfie-style" person looking into the camera is still doing really well for my clients and me. Conversely, if a business has a decent brand and the brand has a face, then going the eye-to-eye, "I see that you didn't buy. I bet it was for this reason. That's not true. Swipe up and buy now," route is less effective; it comes off as aggressive.

Over the past year, Instagram has been hot, especially Story ads. The ROI is ridiculous. Whereas Facebook just rolls out specific new ad options and, in order to get everyone to try them, they make sure that the CPMs are really low when they are first available. For the kind of person that's constantly testing and ends up testing those, that's one way some advertisers are getting advertising ROI.

Personally, I hate having clients jumping from one hot thing to the other. They might be great, but their bread and butter is going to be the news feed. That's where all the inventory is. The ROI might not be as crazy, but that's how they're going to make money on ads every day for the next 8 months.

CURRENT TRENDS

I put a lot of focus on the audience network, retargeting confirmed customers in order to turn them into repeat customers. If a customer added to cart, for the next 3 days I would aggressively retarget that customer in the audience network. My clients and I have slowly been rolling from that high intent retargeting to using Audience Network ads in lower or higher places in the funnel, and it's doing better and better as long as they continue to focus on potential customers who are still open to learning about the product.

We ran into a lot of problems when we were bidding on video views on the Audience Network placement, so I recommend not going that route. But as long as someone is bidding on the purchase conversion, then Facebook is doing a better and better job at drawing in the demographic most likely to respond to the product on the Audience Network. At this point, it doesn't have a ton of volume for us, but the CPAs are great and we're just averaging out the cost of acquiring a customer to lower. As long as we're careful about telling Facebook exactly what we want, Facebook is getting better and better at grabbing those people in the cheapest place possible.

When it comes to recent trends and staying relevant, it's all about creative. Maybe there was a time where you could be lazy about creative and pump out 2-3 pieces a month, but that time is in the past. Now, I recommend lots of creative and, ideally, lots of video in excess. You can cut those different pieces together into something that is engaging, entertaining, and informative, depending on what kind of niche you're in. As you move further and further into using Facebook ads, your ads need to be engaging in some way. Funny, curious, or educational, are all great themes to use to create engagement. The closer you can get to creating great content, the better you will do in the future, as those are the things that Facebook wants: money and for people to stay engaged on the platform forever.

In a world where scrolling through a news feed reveals that every single post is engaging, no one is ever going to leave that platform. Conversely, if the audience sees 3 or 4 things that are engaging from friends, and then 6 or 7 horrible, boring ads that are trying to sell them, it's not a great experience. Ideally, a business should have a great product that solves a problem, and great ads that are engaging in some way. That will become more and more important as time progresses.

There are a few creatives that I like to keep in mind when I'm working with my clients.

Video is what I recommend spending the most time on. Most videos should be shorter than 2 minutes. Once there's a video that does well, though, over time it atrophies and performance decreases. My trick for this is to just change the first 2-5 seconds of the video. The first 2-5 seconds of a video are what I call a scroll stopper. A scroll stopper is a strong image that's interesting enough to have you stop scrolling and wonder what it is. As long as we continue to change that piece, then we see our video creatives lasting a lot longer.

As for the content of the rest of the video, text overlays are a must, as most people don't turn on their volume while they're scrolling. People need to be able to understand what's happening in the ad with the volume off or it's just wasting those impressions that you are paying for.

There is some debate as to whether ads with people in them or animated explainer videos work better. I'm generally in favor of ads with people, but I've seen both types work well. For more complicated products, sometimes animated ads are necessary.

When it comes to creating good creative, ideally it is something related to the product. One of my clients in the sleep niche used a video where the scroll stopper was a rooster crowing in a bed at night, as an example. It's a naturally confusing image, where many things are happening that should not happen. So everyone stops, and there are people who watch about 25% of the video or more. Adding the scroll stopper meant that more people got to that 25% point.

Of course, not everything stays relevant forever. If something was a good idea 1 or 2 years ago, that doesn't mean it still is.

In a general sense, there's just a higher standard now. If a business doesn't have a great product and a great message, it's going to fail. From a high level, if a business is heavily segmenting ad sets and different placements, I don't recommend doing that. It creates more work and ultimately will end up costing more, since it works against the Facebook algorithm. For some clients, when they first started with me, I went from manual placements to automatic placements and just doing that the return on ad spend increased by 30% in their accounts.

It's also important to remember that the people creating the ads are not computers, and thus don't think or behave like computers, and that's an important distinction. There's a human aspect that's important to add to creative. Using a keto product as an example, a person may very well know all the things that people who are on a keto diet want, such as ice cream, and sneaking that into the creative is something that a computer could never do; it would never make that association. Your job as a marketer is to think about things like that and then point Facebook in the right direction to do all the math through their finely-tuned algorithm.

Looking to the near future, I suspect things will become more and more pay-to-play. At the moment, it's a magical era with free traffic and free reach. However, recently there was an article about Instagram slowly but surely deleting the number of likes and the engagement that posts have in Australia. It's a great way for them to make sure that people have to pay to play. No longer can you have a post that gets a ton of engagement that ends up with people getting drawn in because they're curious. Instead, you're going to have to pay for everything that hasn't gone viral, and I suspect that's where things are headed. It's why I put so much emphasis on working on the creative, putting more time into great images and great stories. It's the way to win on Facebook and Instagram, but also elsewhere. The better the creative is, the better it will perform, and not having great creative is going to make everything very difficult.

Discover how the ARM5 Formula has helped companies do $93,000 in one day (138,497% ROAS), $330,000 during Black Friday 2019 (6349% ROAS), $274,000 during Valentine's Day 2019 (1531% ROAS), and an average 1480.61% ROAS throughout 2019 by going to **www.joshmarsden.com/success**

CHAPTER 8

Phil Graham: The Facebook Advertising Whisperer and Creator of the EED Formula

I'm a sales guy. I used to work in corporate America and I was always a sales guy. I was a sales representative and then a sales manager, but I always loved marketing, too. When I had a career in sales I was always marketing as a side hustle. It was fun and I was doing really well at it. Then, there came a point where I needed to make a decision about whether I wanted to start my own agency or keep working for someone else. There's nothing wrong with working for somebody else, but at that point in time, I knew I wanted to direct my own future. I started my own marketing agency 7 or 8 years ago.

Ever since then, things have been going extremely well. I love being able to help entrepreneurs and companies leverage social media paid advertising to attract the kind of customers and clients that they want. I love helping people and companies that do good things for others.

FUNDAMENTAL DIFFERENCES BETWEEN FACEBOOK AND INSTAGRAM ADS

The biggest difference is the audience. On Facebook, you have an older audience. You still have younger people on there, but the age skews much higher on Facebook. On Instagram, the age of the audience skews lower. However, I'm not necessarily talking to generation Z, who might be 15 or 20. Once you get into the 20-35 age range, Instagram is huge. Celebrities are big, too. There are so many people who use Instagram as their primary social media network now. They may or may not use Facebook, too, but Facebook's primary audience is typically a lot higher in age. All ages are on Facebook, but Instagram is the place to be right now if you want to target somebody 25-45.

For Instagram and Facebook, although especially Instagram, we try and go with really short, punchy creatives. We keep them around 5-7 seconds, if we can. It's hard if you're trying to give value in 7 seconds, though. You almost can't say much that's important but you might be able to get their attention in that amount of time. Primarily, Instagram is an image-based social media platform. Videos still work there, but images and very short videos work really well for us.

A lot of people make the mistake of doing the same thing everywhere. They'll use the same content for an ad on Facebook, Instagram, and possibly elsewhere. Sometimes that could work, but if you really narrow your content down for each platform you're going to have more success.

WHAT'S WORKING

For Instagram, we focus on video ads no longer than 15 seconds, and also Stories. I love Story ads. Instagram Stories is one of the primary platforms right now, but you have to be really creative. It can't feel like a sale or a push, but if you can create a successful creative that you advertise in people's Instagram Stories, that could do well for you.

On the Facebook side of advertising, a lot of what's working is video. Short video is working well, although not as short as we would use on Instagram. My favorite length for Facebook video ads is 30-60 seconds. It's short enough that we can still get awareness without people thinking it's too long, but it's long enough that we can get a message out. We can educate. We can inspire somebody. We have enough time to differentiate things. I call them micro-content video ads. We do longer ads, too, but use micro-content for running ads on one specific topic or angle. For example, if you're a gym or a trainer, you would run a short video on building muscle and then you could do a different video on losing weight. You would be able to see who watches and find out what they like and what they don't like. You could retarget based on that. Most people don't do that. They just put out broad, general content and use broad, general retargeting.

A lot of people don't realize that if somebody watches a video ad on Facebook, Facebook knows they watched it even if they don't click on anything or visit your website. You can actually put them into an audience and tell Facebook to give you everybody who watched at least 50% of a particular video. After that, you can send them another ad on that same topic.

I have a formula I call the EED formula: Educate, Entertain, and Differentiate. If we can do all 3 in a video that gives us a good chance of getting whatever result we want. Education can be teaching somebody something, but it doesn't have to be. It could be inspiring them. Similarly, entertaining doesn't necessarily mean you have to act crazy in the video. It could just mean having passion for what you're talking about. Differentiating is about showing how you're different from everything else out there. If you can get those points in a video in an interesting, entertaining way, you have a good chance at succeeding.

I never recommend starting video ads with an introduction. If you don't get to the meat of the ad in 10 seconds, your audience has wandered off again. I recommend starting an ad with something interesting. It could be a question. It could be a bold statement. It just needs to get their attention. In most videos that we use, there's a call to action at the end. If I can fit that into 30-60 seconds, I consider it a success.

I think most people know the "educate" part. As it depends on your product or service, educating could mean many different things. You may or may not be educating people on your exact product. It could be more of an industry education or a complimentary use of the product. There are a lot of different ways you can educate, but a lot of people seem to get stuck on entertaining. They think that they have to be somebody very comfortable on video, but that's not the case. Entertaining could be introducing a prop, such as grabbing your phone while you're on camera. It could even be the location that's entertaining. Entertaining just means getting and keeping their attention.

Share your message with passion, even if it's a "boring" product. There are plenty of boring products out there, but if you're passionate about getting it into the hands of people who could benefit from it, that will show through and, most of the time, that's enough. If that's not enough, there are little things you can do that can help you get more attention in that video. How can you be different? You don't want to be the same as everybody else or you'll never get noticed. The rest of your ad could be great, but you've got to start off with a hook to really grab them at the beginning. If you can do that then you have a good chance of getting them to do what you want.

A hook is a reason why they need to stop and keep watching. For example, I love football and I love the Seahawks. A hook for me would be if you talked about the Seahawks in an ad. That piques my interest. If you just talk about football that probably won't hook me. Talking about something specific that I'm interested in will work much better. If you had a weight loss product, mentioning what it does for you at the beginning of the video is a hook. If you just start talking about features, you don't give anybody a reason to keep watching. A hook is a benefit-driven reason that drives curiosity. The hook could even be something that gets them asking what you're talking about. They'll want to keep listening.

CURRENT TRENDS

The political climate and upcoming elections are always something to consider. They charge the atmosphere, and a lot of people get sick of social media during those periods. That means you need to up your creative game. You need to be the opposite of all that negativity.

One trend I see happening a lot that I really don't like is templated advertising. There are so many people who use these templates and don't put any of their own work into them. They just think if they use a template that they'll be successful. In my opinion, you need to put your own message and brand into it. I'm not going to get the result I want by just quoting someone famous. Even if a template worked for somebody else, you're not their business or their brand. I see a lot of people thinking they can just use something that somebody else uses and they'll automatically be successful. They get frustrated when it doesn't work. If people put the full effort in, they would have so much more success.

I've also noticed a lot of entrepreneurs and advertisers are so focused on trying to optimize their whole business for Facebook likes. I'm not saying they shouldn't, but it shouldn't be the main outcome goal. I've talked to so many people who feel like they're not successful if they don't get a certain number of likes. I know people making $150 million a year who can post a video and they will probably get nothing on it. It doesn't matter. Likes and vanity metrics like that do not equal success. I think sometimes people get that twisted. I'm not saying don't post stuff. I'm just saying don't optimize your whole business's marketing on vanity metrics.

WHAT THE FUTURE HOLDS

There are a number of things people should be doing. First of all, they should be leveraging video ads. I think video ads are the most undervalued way to get your message out in this day and age. They probably will be for another 12-18 months or more. But as time goes on and more companies with big money to spend start putting it into video and social media, the cost will go up eventually. With Google Ads, I used to be able to get mortgage keywords for 5 cents a click. Those same keywords are now $50-$100 a click. Currently, it's still relatively inexpensive to target a market and put a video in front of them on a consistent basis, but it will not always be like that.

Anybody who wants to get a message out needs to adapt. They need to not only put videos out, but do it consistently and with interesting videos that grab attention. Use that EED formula. Use micro-content along with broad content. Retarget people and don't expect that they're going to buy the first time they see you. This is the biggest mistake people make with Facebook ads. You're advertising to people who have never seen you and you're immediately asking for a sale or for an email. It's like walking up to somebody on the street and saying, "Hey, buy my product."

I would walk up to that stranger and start a conversation first. Eventually, it would be the right time to pitch the product. My version of starting a conversation on Facebook is by doing ads that educate, entertain, and differentiate without first going for a sale. Now, there is a caveat to that. If you have an inexpensive eCommerce product, that can be very different. If it's not very expensive, you can run ads and sometimes go straight for the sale. I like to test both and we scale whatever works best. However, typically starting off with some value before you try to get a cold audience to buy something is the best way to go on Facebook.

You also need to give it enough time. People might love what they see, but is the timing right for them to buy it? A lot of times it's not, so retargeting is how you win the game of Facebook ads. Retargeting is where 95% of your sales will come from.

I also see too many people rely on organic reach as a primary way to get customers, and it's a disaster just waiting to happen, even if it's working right now. You can't scale organic reach so you cannot count on it. If you're relying only on organic reach as the primary way to get a customer or client, you're in trouble. Ads give you a system that actually attracts. You direct it to who you want to see it. You're not guessing. If you post organically you don't know how many people are going to see it or who they are. When you do ads, you direct it to specific people and it gives you a system that you can count on for consistency, then scale.

Going along with that, a lot of advertisers look at what other people are doing and do the same things. I try to do the opposite so my ads look and feel different than what most people are doing.

When it comes to eCommerce specifically, I've worked with so many Shopify sites and eCommerce sites that are just selling random products. The great stores are like 1 in 10 million. Typically, I tell them to have a brand around their product or products. You need to have an identity on your site. You need to showcase a reason why somebody would want "Jack's T-shirts" or "Jill's purses." You don't want them just buying the fabric, material, or the t-shirt. You want them to buy into you and your brand. Anytime I consult or take on a client that's eCommerce, the vast majority are not doing that when they come to me. If you can get people to buy from you not just because you have a cool product, but because it's you and what you stand for, you'll stand out. It doesn't matter how many other eCommerce shops there are.

AI and VR are going to be really interesting in the future. We have people who are already learning because it's going to be huge in so many ways that we don't even realize. There are so many new technologies that are coming.

In the future, Facebook and Instagram Advertising are going to get more expensive, but we're in a sweet spot currently. The next 12 to 24 months will be a great time, but there's going to be more ads and more noise, and the "cream" will rise to the top. The people who are super creative and give a lot of value are really going to shine. They're going to have to do it consistently in order to be successful, though.

People need to diversify and utilize more than only Facebook or Instagram ads. Not everybody likes Facebook or has Facebook. There are many who do, but you should also be advertising on Instagram. The reverse is true, too. You should be advertising on YouTube and other social media sites for the same reason. Even so, the opportunity to reach your market on Facebook is still huge. It's going to be amazing for a long time to come, so you need to jump on any new technologies as they develop.

I have a prediction. I think Facebook is going to do a lot more with voice specifically. I predict that in 2020 Facebook will come out with something that lets people do a voice update.

I see voice the way people saw mobile 10 years ago. Facebook was not optimized for mobile before and they've adjusted really well. I believe they're going to do that with voice. Facebook is already getting into your home with the Portal and Oculus Rift products, and there are so many people who are going to get more and more used to searching for things just by talking. I could see Facebook coming out with a voice-specific app that ties into the whole main platform. We're getting into pretty heavy speculation here, though.

EFFECTIVE STRATEGIES

The first one is leveraging an entire system that attracts your ideal customers and turns them into actual paying customers. You're not just running campaigns here and there. You're not just trying out ads for a couple weeks or a month. You're using a system or framework and committing to that consistently. That is the difference between a winner and a loser, and there's a lot that goes into that. You've got to be able to bet on yourself and spend some money to do it. It doesn't have to be a lot of money. You can scale up as you go. However, you should be committed to putting your message out on Facebook, Instagram, and YouTube ads. Leveraging video ads is one of the biggest things we do. If you don't do it, in a couple of years when the 5 or 10 cent video views are $2, you are going to kick yourself for not doing it. Facebook has so many users and so many more advertisers every day that those prices will go up. Leverage it as much as you can and do smart video ads.

Lastly, smart retargeting is the key to your success. We actually do a cool retargeting strategy, which I call an email ad retargeting funnel. Not that many people do this. Let's say you're collecting email addresses. Somebody opts in and you send out an email. Let's say you have 10,000 people on your email list, you send out an email to your list, and 10% open it. Anywhere from 10%-20% is average. That means, out of your 10,000, only 1,000 people opened your email. That means 9,000 did not open it. Maybe they didn't see it. Maybe they didn't like the headline. The fact remains that

9,000 did not open. I'll take the 9,000 that did not open my email, upload them to Facebook as a custom audience, and I'll send them the email as an ad, tweaked a bit so it doesn't look like an email. The final ad is going to be designed to be native for the platform, but it's a way to ensure that you are properly retargeting everything, whether they came from an ad or from email. You can also cap it so they only see it once. It doesn't cost you too much, but also it doesn't annoy the people on your list. We don't do that for every email, though. We reserve it for the important emails, where there's either a lot of extra value or there might be a limited time special offer. If you do that, you can capture so many more sales.

Discover how the ARM5 Formula has helped companies do $93,000 in one day (138,497% ROAS), $330,000 during Black Friday 2019 (6349% ROAS), $274,000 during Valentine's Day 2019 (1531% ROAS), and an average 1480.61% ROAS throughout 2019 by going to **www.joshmarsden.com/success**

CHAPTER 9

Nehal Kazim: Founder of the Cruise Control Method for Facebook Advertising Consistency and Scaling

I run adpros.com. Adpros is an agency and education platform for media buyers, educating both in-house professionals or agencies on how to scale advertising profitably. We are on the eCommerce side, too. Right now, we're managing about $700,000 a month in adspend profitably and we work with high-growth eCommerce companies. That means that they want to grow at least 20%-40% per year, and they want to do it profitably with a scalable front-end offer.

I started out doing websites, trying to figure out how to do anything online because I knew I didn't want to go into traditional work. I knew that being in those more formal structures just wasn't for me. From the first day, I was looking at ways that I could do things myself, and it was hard. I started trying to make money when I was 14 by using eBay. I even started a course on how to play basketball. I didn't even know what I was trying to teach, but I was passionate about basketball. Unsurprisingly, that didn't work.

Eventually, when I was at the University, someone asked me to do a website. I agreed, and it went from there. I did social media marketing services in terms of creating content. Then I saw that being able to reach people through content alone was limited on Facebook and it's even worse now. I knew I needed to "pay to play." I went on to buy a course on Facebook advertising and went through the process. Next, I started successfully selling ad management services at $250 per month. Now, we have clients paying $10,000 or more per month because of the value that we're able to create. It's been a really interesting journey thus far.

I'm 29. I started when I was around 20. I had a really good mentor. His name's Makuch and I still talk to him to this day. He got me into this space and helped me, not just on the agency side, but with how to create it from a strategic standpoint, understanding how to grow it, and designing the agency the way I want it. I learned a lot from him. Eventually, I decided I didn't want to be in Toronto where I grew up. Now, I've been living in different places like Costa Rica and, currently, Medellin, Colombia.

FUNDAMENTAL DIFFERENCES BETWEEN FACEBOOK AND INSTAGRAM

A lot of people, when they're doing ads on Facebook or Instagram, just do auto-placements. That has been changing the game when it comes to delivery and the way ads are performing. However, from what I see, most people stick to Facebook feed, the Instagram feed, or a combination of both, and that's it for their advertising. However, if you look at your Instagram feed right now, you'll see that older stories aren't optimized at all. Sometimes that's okay. What we see is that when we do auto-placements, it works better at this point. Although, in our auto-placement campaigns, we do isolate and optimize for each placement to make sure that the ad creatives are designed for each placement.

For example, the duration of your videos is a big factor. You can't do more than a minute on Instagram. If you're doing carousel ads, we've seen a difference in how those are being perceived and how they're consumed on Instagram vs. Facebook. Whenever Facebook rolls out any advertising feature, they favor it. The CPMs are lower. Usually it's brand new ad inventory, so it means that most people haven't been exposed to it. Usually, it converts higher or it converts better than it will 6 months from the time that they actually launched it.

There are always advertising options that are under-utilized. Right now, Instagram is still relatively under-utilized. Whether you're doing it through your own branded content, or you're doing deals with other Instagram brands, it's a big opportunity right now.

WHAT'S WORKING

For us, there are really 3 main things that are making a difference from a strategic standpoint. Tactics will keep changing and I think that's the exciting part of Facebook ads. Facebook is not for you if you're looking for stable, consistent, predictable performance from an ad platform. When it comes to principles and strategies, the things that we're looking at right now are the rhythms of the account. This is such a difficult part to look at if you don't actively manage your account or if it's not a priority for you, because you don't have a pulse on the account.

We're seeing this frequently in accounts where, when we would expect a specific ratio of ad spend to revenue, it keeps changing. Consider if you normally spend $500 or $1,000 and you're already expecting $1,500 or $2,000 in revenue, but you're not getting that anymore by 9:00 and you don't know what to do. Is it the ads? Is it the ad optimization? Is it the funnel or competition? Is it the delivery? There are so many different factors and the reality is, if you just watch your account, sometimes it just gets delayed by 2 to 3 hours. The same numbers you were expecting by 8:00 or 9:00, now you're expecting them at 11:00 or 12:00. This changes your automated rules, how you're going to make decisions, and the way that you're looking at your performance in your business if Facebook is a big part of it.

The first part we're really looking at is the rhythm of the account. The way to actually look at this is to look at notable months. If there's a really successful month and if there's a really bad month, you compare those to the current month. You can go to the account level and look at the distribution and the breakdown per hour. You can see where the ad spend is coming from, where you have your best CPA, and where you have your best ROAS. For the best months, bad months, and this month, you can see if there's a trend or not.

There are so many variables in the actual inputs compared to the process and the output of Facebook ads. You can only control so much of it. You can have no impact, no input, no adjustments you make that day, but everything can still change. That's a very frustrating and challenging part of being a media buyer. You have to do the assessment. You have to do the analysis. You have to dig deep.

To facilitate this, I would go to Ads Reporting. Facebook Analytics is its own beast, and you have to have it fully set up. Most people get overwhelmed with data, so they aren't able to make any decisions. They feel trapped and even more overwhelmed, so they don't do anything. The opposite of that is going to a section called Ads Reporting, in the drop-down menu when you go into the Ads Manager. When you click it, there are custom columns you can create, but what you are able to do is create the same custom columns that you're doing in the Ads Manager. You can break down the main metrics that are important to you. Your main metrics might be the number of link clicks, the cost per link click, the number of Add to Carts, the cost per Add to Cart, the number of purchases, the cost per purchase, the value of purchase, and ROAS.

You're also able to add filters. What that means is that you're able to set it up to see, for example, every campaign, ad set, or ad that has higher than a 150% ROAS or 250% ROAS. Let's say that your average is 200%; this allows you to see the best of the best. Then you can also set it up to see, for example, campaigns, ad sets, or ads that have a minimum of $500 or $1,000 spend. What that does is give you a vision. We saw this with one of our accounts where we were able to isolate specific types of ads. They were anywhere between $30-$40 more than our targeted CPAs, but it wasn't so apparent in the Ads Manager. What we had to do is go at the campaign level, the ad set level, and the ad level to see what was working. I know it sounds complicated but when you actually go into Ads Reporting, you can set up just the columns that are important to you. You can then look at and manipulate the data very easily. That's a really beginner way to start looking at your data to start making decisions.

(This is why you need to read the bonus chapter at the end with Scott Desgrosseilliers of Wicked Reports.)

The one caveat I would add is that if any of this feels overwhelming, the challenge I would present to you is to figure out how you can take the emotion out of it. For people who struggle with numbers, they're overwhelmed to the point that they freeze up, and that's okay. But as a business owner, as a marketing manager, as the media buyer, you can't be scared of numbers. I used to struggle with this. I knew everyone else's numbers except mine. But I can't be the media buyer or a business owner and know everyone else's numbers but not mine. Now we're working on all the different types of numbers from a business health standpoint. All that only comes out if you're actually confronting what you're scared of. In this case, if numbers freak you out, now's the time to work on that.

On the Instagram side of things, we do Instagram polls. I see them working well for us. I wish I had a profound explanation of why Instagram polls work. The odd thing is that they want people to engage with the poll and then they want people to swipe up. What we're doing is looking at challenges people have from whatever their problem is, asking them a question with 2 options on what their actual challenge is, and asking them to then swipe up. In a physical product example, we're saying, "Which one do you like better?" and they're choosing a product in a poll. In another example, if it's one product, we may ask something like, "Is this hotter or not?" and then swipe up to check it out. We're also doing industry-specific problems. We have to ask ourselves, "What is the challenge the industry has? What is the challenge they specifically have? What are the product-specific quizzes or polls that we can create?" We try different ones and see what works.

CURRENT TRENDS

From an overall platform standpoint, one of the things that we're struggling with is that, in early 2019, what was working very well was the "day-trading model." We were making adjustments on the ad account all the time, manually or automated. We were able to scan 2-4 times per campaign ad set level on each work day. We would set up a bunch of ads and find winners to bump their budgets and see what worked, and scale them that same day. We were able to take accounts from $100 a day to $5,000 a day profitably in a short period of time. That was only because whatever was going on in the platform happened to work at that moment. Now, it's not working as well anymore. One of the challenges I've seen, especially if you're following Facebook ad strategies from random Facebook groups or from very different mindsets, is that trying to do everything you pick up on messes up the delivery and the quality of the account. People are combining ad account ad strategies in the same account to a fault. For people who do this, you're basically guaranteed not to have stability in your account, then traffic quality and conversion rates go down.

Instead, what we're doing is isolated in different accounts. Before, if you created a new account, it would be the end of the world because you needed to warm up that ad account. Now, we're actually creating cruise control accounts, where it's $500-$1,000 a day on cruise control. We just set it and forget it. We're monitoring it, but we're not actively managing it.

On the Instagram side of things, we do a bunch of things. We can provide our cruise control strategy. The problem is identifying what the actual actively tested and managed Ad Campaigns are. What are all the Ad Campaigns that you're not going to move? Typically, when people use our cruise control strategy, they identify these Ad Campaigns, and then decide to move them all at once during testing. We call these ad stacks, and there are specific types of combinations that work. We're testing them across thousands of dollars per day. By now, we've launched 3 cruise control accounts. Two of them are $500-$1,000 a day, and they're outperforming their previous "core" account. These are not designed to scale or to push, but they are designed to create stability and scale more horizontally than vertically within one Facebook ads account.

There are no rules set up on the account and we are sharing pixels within the account. We're isolating CBO (campaign budget optimization) vs. ABO (ad set budget optimization) in our ad campaigns. At this point, a lot of ABO is working. We're taking the best performing types of campaigns or targeting and putting them into these cruise control ad accounts. One example is that after we've identified targeting that's working for us in an ABO campaign, we now have 1 CBO campaign with 5 ad sets. That could mean 2 lookalike audiences that are already proven, 2 interest audiences that are already proven, and 1 broad, open audience. We've seen, even when we're marketing specifically for women in our ad creatives, that when we add men to the mix, the Facebook pixel directs traffic to women. Those are some of the steps we take in our cruise control campaign strategy.

The other decisions that we're making have to do with what frequency we're bumping and increasing the bid. We don't just want to stay at $300 a day. That's just the budget in an ad set in the main account. That's not impressive. We're trying to figure out what the limits are on each account for performance. We love to have $1,000-$5,000 per day. If we can get to about $10,000 per day on cruise control accounts, that's the dream. Diversifying the risk, not only with multiple ad accounts in a Business Manager, but also ideally with additional Facebook pages, is where I think the future of self-branded content and partnerships with 3rd-party brands for lead gen or traffic deals are headed.

There are phases of using cruise control accounts. We realized that with some accounts, when we spend $5,000-$10,000 per day. We hit the upper limits in the account and we don't know what they are. For some accounts, it's as low as $1,000-$3,000 and the account goes completely off the rails. If we were just managing 1 account we could safely assume it's something we're doing that's limiting it, but we have a variety. We have the ability to see across many different accounts, different offers, and different price points. We can see some of the trends. When we're looking at this, we have to ask what's stopping these accounts. We want stability, but there's so much contradicting advice. We're trying to figure out how we manage variables, so the first thing we do, when we find the thing that works, is avoid breaking it. That's such an easy trap because if it's working, what are the things you can actually do to break it? We try to isolate those, and we only move over to these cruise control accounts after we have a base and we already have things working.

MOVING FORWARD

When it comes to how things will progress moving forward, there are expectations at 3 levels.

The first is when it comes to creatives vs. optimizations. We're working so much more heavily on the creative side. We've done Facebook ads for 5 years now. We've launched thousands of campaigns. Everything is working primarily off of stock photos and based off of assets some clients would give us. However, the standard and the performance system inside of Facebook is changing. In the past, you would want to find and use winning Facebook posts, using their IDs, and create the "perfect ad" that would last forever. It's possible, but it's very difficult. We're now seeing that we get rewarded by the more ads we create, even if they're variations. We have zero social proof on that, but we're still able to get the same CPA and ROAS, if not better, just by doing creating new ads at a steady frequency. We actually have clients where we're creating 2-4 new ad assets every week and launching them for campaigns or ad sets that are tapering off performance-wise. The first thing every advertiser and company needs to do is change the expectation that to get great performance, it's not from crazy optimization but it's in investing in ad creatives. The best performance today is not in media-buying magic as much. You'll hit walls. It's all about the creative.

The second thing is that the expectation on ROAS needs to decrease a little bit. It's going to get harder. Of course you can have higher ROAS, but it depends on the growth curve that you're on and the risk tolerance that you have. For us, the majority of people want to be on a growth curve of 30%-40% growth per year. If you're doing that, there's so much going on and so much to keep track of at the same time. When you grow that quickly, you're going to have plateaus with your team. You're going to have plateaus with ad spend. You're going to have plateaus mentally as the entrepreneur, the marketing person, or the media buyer. Everything is going to break. You're going to have issues with fulfillment, chargebacks, and customer service. If you actually want hyper-growth, the expectation has to change from the backend.

The third part of it is that you want the conversions and the CLTVs to be way higher on the backend. Our most profitable clients have this. I'm not talking about just Facebook advertising being profitable. I'm talking about the business in terms of gross margin, the profit margin of what they actually take home. That's making the biggest difference with our clients' success. Every business running Facebook Ads should be focused on elevating these standards.

As a whole, though, ads can be nerve-wracking. They take time. Other reliant systems and processes could break. Even so, there's always a time to be aggressive about it if you're a growth-minded company. If you look at the average media buyer, they're very complacent, especially when things work. If you're focused on profit, this is a very different conversation. We're designed for scale. Companies bring us in for that. How we make decisions is about front-end scale so we get to backend profitability. Backend profitability also means selling more within your company and creating additional customer value so you can show growth. There are many different factors here. For us, we're in the mindset of scaling and front-end growth. When you're doing that, I think it's just how you're making those decisions. If you're only spending $1,000 or $5,000 or $10,000 a month, it's not so much about how many graphics you need. I think you should constantly try and beat your control, or beat your best version. When things are working, be even more aggressive and create more graphics. You should test 2-4 graphics a month at minimum, even if they're small variations of existing ad assets.

As entrepreneurs, as a marketing person, or as a media buyer, you're always testing just for the sake of testing. A lot of the time we ask ourselves why we made a decision and why we keep making the same decision even if things aren't working. Setting aside time to think allows you to actually stop and focus on that question. What you'll realize is that the majority of the questions you're asking and the filter you're looking at in your business or media are probably not healthy.

A mistake that I see a lot of people make is making same-day decisions based off of their end-of-month analyses. If today you're spending money and it's not hitting specific benchmarks, but you're actually looking at what happened a month or 2 months ago, and you're looking at Facebook numbers, what you need to realize is that there's delayed attribution. What delayed attribution means is that pixels are going to fire much later because people did their own customer journey and eventually bought, then Facebook attributed that sale to you. Whether that's true or not, there's delayed attribution. If you were to remember that day 2 months ago, you would notice that number is 30%-70% higher. We actually track all of this on a daily basis, automatically and manually. We're tracking end-of-day ROAS and then we're looking at the differential between end-of-day ROAS and dynamic ROAS as we progress. This means that we can see that, after 5 days, it's normally in the range of 10%-50%. Then, for whatever reason, it's 60%. When we're looking at that, looking at the difference actually being 60% 30 days from now, how do we make our decision today? This might actually cost us so much business because we're not looking at it like that. The lesson here is don't make same-day decisions based on data from 30 days ago.

Another tip is that when things are broken, try to understand what's actually happening in the account. It's very easy to make assumptions on what the media buyer's doing, what the marketing person's doing, or what the agency you're working with is doing. It's very easy to judge them, call them out, fire them, and go to the next person. Sometimes it's you and it's really hard to admit, but maybe the way you're making decisions is not good for your business. On the other hand, maybe it's too much trust in the media buyer or the marketing team isn't helping because Facebook is the biggest lever, but you're not asking any questions, poking around, or supporting them. It's easier to keep blaming others, but that creates a lot of resentment. You're not going to be able to scale, be as profitable, sell, or achieve your goals.

Another tip is to not make decisions based off of a profit margin or gross margin of your business on Facebook. There are Facebook-specific numbers and then there are backend business performance numbers. It's very hard to separate them, but you shouldn't make all of your decisions based on how much money the business is making. I think a good way to do it is to have a flat percentage based off of company revenues. You need a clear decision-making framework moving forward.

EFFECTIVE STRATEGIES

We like to break the patterns of ad creatives that people do. Most people create the same type of ad creative, optimize one thing, and just keep optimizing. I think that makes sense until campaigns are broken or you're not seeing a breakthrough in your ROAS or your CPA. The first thing we try to do is change the type of ad creative completely to shock the system and see if we're able to break through. It's a higher risk, but it's also a higher reward if it does work. Then I would make sure we're just doing the normal thing from a creative standpoint, rather than something outside of what's actually working. It might not sound very prescriptive or tactical, but it makes a big difference. It's human nature to be habitual, whether it's positive or negative. But to have big leaps in ROAS, you have to dramatically change things. Ads are one of them.

Automated rules are also a big part of what we do. Where the future is going is less about automated rules, but for some accounts, it is working. What I would look at is turn-off and turn-on rules. You can only manage Facebook ads so much and sometimes ads are going to spend too much money too quickly. These are just protection mechanisms for when anything goes off the rails. The cutoff rule is that if you spend more money than your target CPA, turn ad sets off. The other opportunity is with delayed attribution of when a sale comes in later on. Turn the ad on so that you can still make the most of the day. That makes a difference for us. I wish that auto-scaling with automatically changing bids was working as much as it used to, but I think it can still work in some situations, even if the future is going away from that.

The last thing I would say is, if you're already spending $1,000-$5,000 a day and you feel like you keep hitting these walls in your account, set it up in a way so that it's in your Business Manager but under a different account. Facebook has said that if you have Facebook pages that are separate and set up in separate ad accounts, you're not competing in the same auction. Even if you have multiple ad accounts and you're setting up different targeting, if you have just the one Facebook page, you're still competing in that same ecosystem. But when you have different Facebook pages, you have a clean slate. I think if you can partner with like-minded companies in your industry or brands that you have relationships with, those partnerships are really valuable. We have a consulting client spending $20,000 a month on these cruise control accounts. They're making some adjustments, but they're doing it completely with a separate Facebook page, with a separate Business Manager, and an ad account that's using a big page. This isn't an amateur page either. It's a proper brand from which they actively manage, engage, and run ads through. This is on a separate brand from their usual and they're seeing incredible results on cold ads.

*Discover how the ARM5 Formula has helped companies do $93,000 in one day (138,497% ROAS), $330,000 during Black Friday 2019 (6349% ROAS), $274,000 during Valentine's Day 2019 (1531% ROAS), and an average 1480.61% ROAS throughout 2019 by going to **www.joshmarsden.com/success***

CHAPTER 10

Mari Connor: The Queen of Facebook Advertising the RIGHT Way

I'm the owner of Marigold Marketing Group, a full-service Facebook ads agency that specializes in lead gen and expert marketing. However, there's a portion of our clientele that does fit into the eCommerce space, as well as a little bit of local advertising. We've been doing it since 2012. We're not fly-by-night. We've got an entire US-based team full of thought leaders and thinkers. There's a lot of problem-solving when it comes to Facebook ads, funnels, and where things may be working or not. I'm an implementer and a mechanic when it comes to personality, rather than the star who jumps in front of the camera. My head is usually down at the computer or I'm having meetings with my teams, talking about how we can make campaigns better, solve problems we might be facing, or help our clients increase their ROI.

FUNDAMENTAL DIFFERENCES BETWEEN FACEBOOK AND INSTAGRAM

On the surface level, we're seeing a little bit of an age gap. It's going to be young, earlier adopters, spending more time on Instagram. That's changing rapidly, though. Facebook, despite the issues that they've had, is still the standard name and brand that people trust and are familiar with. They're familiar with the layout, how to behave, and how to interact. They've been trained to some extent, so that's still where we see the bulk of our Instagram activity. For Facebook, it seems to be mainly the 35 and older demographic. For this demographic, they have more disposable income and are interested in higher-ticket offers. In general, Facebook is where they're going to be.

Instagram plays a bigger role when it comes to new, young, stylish users. The mom and mom-preneur communities are growing over there and I think they're pulling a little bit of market share from Pinterest. We're still in a place where we definitely test both. On any given campaign or any given account, Instagram will outperform Facebook and vice versa.

What really works with Facebook ads is leading with benefits. You can't just start out the pitch-fest when you're promoting anything. There has to be a customer journey. A number of online influencers are proponents of patience as a value for entrepreneurs, and it's going to become more important. Eventually it will be the differentiator between a successful brand and an unsuccessful brand. You'll need patience in terms of spending the time to set up, develop, and build something true, rather than a hack used solely to get people over to your profile to follow you. That's selfish, ultimately, and people are able to sniff that out more and more.

Be authentic about your brand and to your audience. Be yourself in all aspects of your life, whether it's on your personal profile or your business profile. Take the audience through a customer journey. Introduce them to a little bit of free content, be it blogs, videos, or something else. Get them to interact with or like your page. Wait until they've had a little bit of an initiation to your brand before you start pitching your wares. What's ironic is that everything I'm saying is intuitive in all of us. We know that we don't like that "smarmy" person at the dinner party who leads with the fact that he's an insurance agent and could help us out. You want a relationship first. You want to get a bit of advice first. If you end up taking that advice and getting a quick win from it, that makes you remember that person, brand, or product.

The benefits of this approach go both ways. You stand to make a higher level of ROI on all of the energy that you put in during the relationship-building phase, mixed with what you spend and invest in the pitch to closing phase. You'll get a much higher ROI on all of that, compared to trying to pitch right away.

Let's say you've invested $10,000 to build a landing page, create a Facebook page, and have an offer to make, using Facebook ads. You want to come into Facebook, make your money, and get out. You run that, and you may luck out. You stand to make maybe 1.5 to 2 times ROI on that $10,000, in my experience. On the other hand, if you spend a year, investing $50,000 over that year, you stand to make 4 or 5 times ROI just by showing that you care and by helping people first.

We have to keep in mind how we want to be treated when we're consumers ourselves. How do we behave when we think about the purchases we make? We don't make fast buys. We take our time. We do research. Why would we expect the audience we're marketing toward to be any different? So let's help them do their research. Let's help point them in the right direction so they're learning the key points that they need to know.

Over on the Instagram side of things, Stories are taking off. We want to lead with the idea that swiping up is going to enhance their lives, they're going to learn something, or we can help if there's something that they need help with. We don't want to just flash a sale out of nowhere for a product that may or may not apply to their lives or the stage of buying that they're at.

On any given campaign, it's up in the air whether a campaign is performing better on the Facebook feed, the Instagram feed, or Instagram Stories. We choose all placements, and we let Facebook optimize for us at this point. We study the results and get an idea, in each ad account, of which one tends to lean toward the Facebook feed, the Instagram feed, or Instagram Stories. We want to be everywhere, wherever we're getting the results that we want, whether that's a lower cost, a high immediate ROI, a high customer value, or a higher retention.

We use a mix of Facebook's best practices, what we know in the short-term to have worked, and what has worked in the long-term. That's why we have so many team meetings. We're hashing out what trends we're seeing and testing them. There are times when launching a campaign and managing the budget at the ad set level delivers much higher ROI, so we stick with that as opposed to moving to the new campaign budget optimization option.

CURRENT TRENDS

Diversification and making sure that you always have a nice mix of advertising that's warming cold traffic up with helpful content, that's big right now in ads. Making sure that you're taking those people who you've introduced to your brand with content and continuing to warm them is just as important. If they've seen a video, make sure that they get an offer to visit your website or blog with a hook that the action will solve one of their problems. Try to hit them as many times as you can, because we do see a significant differentiator in ROI between warm traffic (people who have been introduced to your brand at least once) and hot traffic (people who have been to your website recently and visited multiple types of content).

For things to work well, a company's owner and the marketing manager need to be part of the conversation about what's going on. As implementers, we need to know what's working throughout their business. If they're sending out mailers or doing some Google advertising that's working, we want to know and be able to report to them what's working on the Facebook ads side, so they can take that to other aspects of their business. We need everybody to compare notes on what isn't working so we're not continuing to do that. In general, we believe in doing 80% of what's working and 20% of testing new ideas, new taglines, and new offers. One of those is going to become part of the 80% in the future. That way, when clients are saying they want to test a bunch of different things, I can guide them in maintaining a healthy business, and I can ensure they're taking notes on what's been working.

(This is why you need to read the bonus chapter at the end with Scott Desgrosseilliers of Wicked Reports.)

Within the last year specifically, Facebook has developed an even lower threshold for overly aggressive, over-promising flashy words or taglines that don't deliver a result that the average Facebook user can achieve. Things like, "Let me show you how to go from 0 to 7 figures in a certain amount of time." You want to make it a bit more specific yet complex, without promising a certain result within a certain timeframe. Something more like, "Let me show you the 3 changes you need to make in your business to be able to scale to 7 figures and beyond." You're tweaking it to make it slightly abstract, but staying away from overly aggressive language.

We're hearing and seeing more reports of disabled accounts, and I imagine a lot of that is coming from the scrutiny that Facebook has taken part in. From their perspective, they're doing just fine on the advertising and profit side, so there's not one specific advertiser they need to keep on board, including big brands. Whatever you're spending on Facebook ads, it really is a drop in the bucket to them. It behooves you to maintain the relationship and to remain a non-aggressive good advertising citizen within the Facebook advertising community.

Another thing is to be careful about where information comes from. We'll have clients coming to us with lists of contact information, saying they bought it from a third party data source or pulled it from LinkedIn. That sort of thing is going to become absolutely toxic to your online existence. If a client shares with us that they're uploading a list that they did not collect in a 100% compliant way, we won't have anything to do with that. I won't put it past Facebook to be rating or monitoring our behavior as an agency, so make sure your lists are fully compliant and that you're getting people to opt-in the right way.

You also want to make sure you hire a decent copywriter. You need to double-check everything. There are multiple ways to say the same thing and you want to make sure you're saying it in the best, most compliant way. You want to filter your copy through Facebook policy compliance. My team is assigned to read the Facebook policies a minimum of once a week because new ones are thrown in there without any fanfare or announcement.

WHAT THE FUTURE COULD HOLD

What I'm sensing as we're creating ads is that we're making them a lot more authentic. We used to set up campaigns so that branded images, typically the person behind the brand, the product, or the logo, would go out to warm audiences. More generic photos would go out to cold audiences. Now, we're getting away from graphics that are just using photos. If you can use photos of the person who represents the brand, that's wonderful. Now, to do this, we're asking clients not just for photoshoot photos, but a file of socially acceptable photos of themselves that they like and appreciate. This leads us to making ads that look like they're genuine and authentic posts.

Facebook is slowly starting to remove targeting here and there. We need to be prepared for the possibility of them pulling a lot of interest targeting away from us, or limiting the types of lookalikes that we can use. The one place where you're still going to be able to do targeting, no matter what, is copy. You need to be able to write copy that uses words, phrases, and languages that are inside of the heads of your ideal prospects. What are they thinking? How would they refer to you, your service, and your product? You have to figure out the specific language that your tribe uses around your product. You can use that as a way to sift through the audience on Facebook and as a way to do subtle callouts without announcing, "Attention so-and-so."

The writing is on the wall, and you can see Facebook pulling away more and more. There was a day when everybody was so excited to announce that on Facebook you can target the 38-year-old woman who loves broccoli in this zip code. Well, that 38-year-old woman who loves broccoli in that zip code is annoyed that you can find her now. She's bothered and feels like her privacy is being compromised. All we can do is look to what other mediums are doing in their content and targeting to sift and filter ideal prospects. I'm referring to mediums like radio, TV, print, and so on. The main way you sift through the demographic to find the one that you want is by the content that they put out.

EFFECTIVE STRATEGIES

One would be telling stories and making your posts more authentic, genuine, and approachable. Your business posts should mimic the personal posts that you see on social media. Whatever platform you're advertising on, make sure that your advertising is in line with what's actually going on in the news feed that you're seeing. It can't be a pattern interrupt when they see your ad. You want it to be extraordinarily natural. Another strategy to consider that works really well is using the voice of the brand and his or her business influencer profile, so it's a person's name that's going through someone's newsfeed with an advertisement. It's more natural to see a post from Mari Connor as opposed to Marigold Marketing Group. Marigold Marketing Group is immediately going to be a pattern interrupt.

There are 2 ways to put a story together. One would be to interview one of our actual customers and perhaps offer them discounts or compensation for their time. We could say, "Meet David. He's 39. He bought our product because of _____ (this reason)," then set up some interview questions that help him speak to some of the objections that other potential customers might have. That would be the easiest way, because then you don't have to do a lot of thinking or copywriting yourself. You're letting David provide the language. So maybe find a top buyer or a superfan of the brand. If you can't get your own David, another way is doing how-to videos. You could do a 3-5 minute video to answer a question a potential customer might have. There are recommendations to record small videos, but I feel like if you have something to say, you can say it. One minute or less if you think you can get it in and do some editing. But if not, even up to 3 or 5 minutes is fine, provided you're talking about something that's helpful to your audience.

Another strategy is for eCommerce specifically. Make sure that Facebook ads will not solve a bad marketing problem. Make sure that, before you start running ads, your website and product pages are completely optimized to convert traffic. Make sure that you have the opportunity for visitors to sign up for an email list if they aren't ready to buy. Make sure that you have your pixel installed and can retarget audiences that land on the website, or the product page, or the Add to Cart page. Have an Add to Cart or an Abandoned Cart sequence set up. You would be shocked at how many eCommerce and retail businesses don't have an Abandoned Cart email sequence set up. It's the lowest hanging fruit. They were almost there, but they had one objection that you need to be able to handle, and being able to send them a series of emails that perhaps address that one objection is important. Keep in mind, Facebook ads will not solve an offer problem, a funnel problem, or a poor marketing problem. Facebook ads are amazing at amplifying what you might have tested in the market that has worked. We won't take on clients where Facebook ads are their "Hail Mary," meaning a desperate play to get results.

Just like ad accounts, every business is a little bit different. Starting out, the conversion percentages are going to be fairly low, but it's going to be different levels of low from one business to another. I would say anywhere between 1% and 10% depending on your business. Then your goal, if your conversion rate is now .5%, is 1%. You'll have to tweak the offers that you're making, the copywriting that you're using, and the customer journey that you're sending them on through your website to increase conversion. You have to test and tweak each one to see if each page can increase the conversion rate so that the overall conversion rate of the website is approaching 1%. Once you hit 1%, celebrate. Enjoy the moment. Then, set a new goal of 1.5%. Study other business owners that are in the same industry to find what an optimal rate is and let that be a compass. However, don't feel like you have to stick to it. There's no reason you can't go over it if you want to but just slapping together a website with very basic graphics and a terrible mobile experience won't cut it. I've opted into multiple companies' email opt-ins and not received anything but a thanks. If someone goes to your website and goes to the effort of opting-in, that's one step down from being a buyer. They invested their personal information and their time. They just haven't invested money.

The next strategy is to have fun. Be yourself. Give your brand a personality. If your brand is one-dimensional, your audience is going to sniff that out. Find someone who is a superfan of your products to perhaps be the voice in your Facebook groups and in your email. Bring them into your team. Find a way to do some sort of product compensation, financial compensation, or a full-on partnership. Be open to partnering with someone who can give your business that second dimension. The third dimension would be a mission that is in line with what your product is doing, and that's the gold. Find a mission that's related to your brand, but not to you if you're not a superfan of the products you use. Find that superfan. Make sure that they have a voice and that they're the one who is speaking to your audience. Filter your business acumen through them. They can give the brand a personality and find a mission that's bigger than just the product.

Discover how the ARM5 Formula has helped companies do $93,000 in one day (138,497% ROAS), $330,000 during Black Friday 2019 (6349% ROAS), $274,000 during Valentine's Day 2019 (1531% ROAS), and an average 1480.61% ROAS throughout 2019 by going to **www.joshmarsden.com/success**

CHAPTER 11

John Hutchison: One of the Pioneers of E-Commerce and Master Facebook Alchemist

I've been really working with Facebook ads since late 2009, so it's been a little while. My exposure started from getting into eCommerce and selling physical products online first. Over the years I've ventured deeper into Facebook ads and learning how to run ads for lead generation, online event registrations, selling service-based products, and selling physical products. In terms of my background, I started my first eCommerce store back in 2004. It took me over a year to get it going. Back then the landscape was a little bit different. You had to import and you had to have your own little warehouse. There wasn't dropshipping going on back then. Plus, the other thing that I got wrong and figured out after about a year was that coming from an IT background, I could build an online store quite well. However, after I opened the store I would just refresh and refresh, waiting for sales. I completely overlooked the whole traffic thing.

That's when my traffic research began. I went down the slippery slope of SEO, got caught up in Google's Panda search algorithm, and so on. I ditched SEO in 2009 and decided the way to go was paid traffic with online advertising. The reason to go paid was that you were in more control of the traffic, so my whole mindset changed, in that the only way to go was paid traffic.

EARLY LESSONS

The biggest thing is to continue learning through education what you're trying to master. The technology and things like the algorithms that they're using across these platforms are forever changing and getting better, so you have to keep up with those changes or you're going to get left behind. I'm always looking to see who's doing what, to reverse engineer what they're doing, and try to figure out if it has a weakness.

Always be up-to-date with things as much as possible, but you also have to test your way to success. Because everything with online marketing changes so fast, every time you put something out there, it's a brand new test. You have to leverage that data to get insightful information, because once you've got some historical data you can then see valuable trends. If you know how to interpret data correctly you can make predictions to eliminate the risk and look to get a better return.

FUNDAMENTAL DIFFERENCES BETWEEN FACEBOOK AND INSTAGRAM

First, it's a slightly different demographic. The second thing is in the actual information that's being presented. Instagram is now a crowd of people who want instant gratification: the people who are constantly on their phones and love to share things.

Whereas the people on Instagram are generally a little bit younger than the crowd on Facebook, Facebook is now an older demographic than what it used to be in the beginning. The style of message that's being delivered over that type of medium is different, too. Facebook really is the social platform for sharing and having longer discussions, while Instagram is more swipe-ups and seeing what's going on.

We're seeing the people who now adopt Instagram are a slightly different type of person. They're definitely a younger crowd, as there are more millennials using it now. But they're using it more like instant messaging as opposed to Facebook. Instagram has come a long way since its inception, but it's a very different platform. It's focused on short bursts of fast information, as opposed to slower conversations that are happening on Facebook.

Instagram is a very image- and video-based medium. You have to deliver value, but you can do it while putting out really engaging posts. You're trying to deliver value, but it's very visual. If you have a visual of your product, say beauty products for example, that's where Instagram is completely different from Facebook.

The biggest things that we really have working are the testing mechanism and the creatives. The creatives pretty much form 75% of our results. If you get the creative right, then it works for you. It doesn't matter if it's a service or physical product business. Even so, you have 2 things that you need to get right. A big thing now with Facebook is the overall user experience. Where we used to just put images of products or images of T-shirts and get interest, now you have to think, "What's the outcome of the product?" If you've heard the phrase, "Sell the sizzle, don't sell the steak," that's pretty relevant right now. If you can get engagement and relevance, then you are awarded in terms of the Facebook advertising auction or in the performance through the platform's algorithm. By doing this and focusing on an overall user-centric experience in your advertising, you're going to get a better quality score. For example, let's compare apples to apples. You've got advertiser A and advertiser B, with the same bidding strategy. If A is generally giving a better user experience, though, then A is going to win more auctions and more ad traffic. Winning more auctions gets you in front of the audience against your competition.

When you're working with engagement or relevance, you win the auction. Secondly, you're going to get better click-through rates. If you get better click-through rates then you'll get cheaper per-click costs as well.

WHAT WORKS

The first thing you have to do is think of who the ideal customer is. What's the persona of the ideal customer? You need to understand this first by gender. Generally, men and women react differently. The other thing is the age range and how you talk to people. If you think about young people, they may use more slang than older people. You have to understand who you're talking to so you get the relevance of the message correct. Trying to target someone who's 20 and male vs. someone who's female and 55 will require completely different types of creatives and copy in relation to their underlying reasons for wanting to engage.

When it comes to Instagram, Stories or posts with very short creatives and videos that capture the attention within the first 3 seconds are key. You're essentially trying to stop the scroll right away. While doing that, though, many businesses try and put too much emphasis on what they're trying to do. People get lost in trying to sell the product. They have to slow down. The end goal is, obviously, to sell the end product. However, your ad has one job: it has to stop the scroll and get the click to get people to your own real estate. People get lost in that and end up making their creatives over-complicated and too long. On Facebook, we tend to have about a 30-second video, while on Instagram we aim for 10 to 15 seconds. A video's sole job is to get the click. Once you have the click, you have someone's interest. Once you have the interest, you have to work more on the actual engagement and getting people to the next step.

The majority of people, when they start, try to get very specific with their targeting. Obviously, that's for a reason. They think they don't want to attract everyone, because not everyone is their ideal customer. However, the problem with that is that CPMs (cost per 1,000 impressions) go up the more targeted you are. Facebook's not silly. They understand that if there's a very small segment of people and you really are targeted in, then the cost is going to be higher. So one of the things that we do is make sure that, within our ad and our copy, it is really focused on speaking to the ideal persona we're trying to attract. We get this down to the gender and the age-range in the creative. We want to get that person to be aware and the copy needs to draw them in. However, the copy has to filter people out too. The big thing is to try and repel as much as you attract. Not everyone is your ideal prospect or customer. Therefore, you'll find that you get a cheaper CPM rate. Plus, if you get a good click-through-rate, you end up getting cheaper clicks. After the click, you have to continue that verification and filtering process.

We use a lot of presale pages to get the initial awareness and engagement. We're winning auctions and getting cheap traffic. We've designed the ad to filter people, weeding out the people it's not really for. We really are speaking to the right person with the right pain point who is looking for a solution to their problem. Therefore, once we get them past the presale page, we know that's the targeted group of prospects that we are after. We've filled the funnel and then we do the whole filtering process. You build better audiences and, more importantly, you get a higher conversion as a result. We're buying less targeted traffic, but we're making sure that we filter those people. Then we can use those audiences to build better targeted audiences to expand.

We like to use narrative stories where, initially, we give them 1 page of the book or magazine, and once they've read that, they want to consume more. Then we take them through that next stage and give them more value. That's how you filter out people, but if they continue reading, you know you've caught the right prospect. You've got them on the hook and you've started to reel them in.

Once we get them to the page, we're obviously going one step at a time. As they take the next step, the audience becomes a little bit smaller, but it becomes a lot warmer. As they go deeper, those audience members have been dealt with. What we like to do is use Google Tag Manager to run a tag to fire the pixel based on various actions and behaviors. We start to learn a lot of different information as people become warmer and warmer. Using GTM, we like to create lists based on, for example, bounce time. We exclude those people who bounce within the first 10 seconds in our advertising further down the funnel. Other examples can also be time on the page, whether they scrolled down, if they clicked a particular button, and so on. The deeper they go, the more they navigate, meaning the more we know they're interested.

You can also build lists based on how long people stay on your site. Someone who stays 7 minutes, as opposed to 1 minute, is much hotter. They're reading through every piece of information. On one of our particular projects, the average timeframe is 7 minutes. That's a massive amount of time and an extremely hot list that we're creating.

We utilize the actual makeup of that to create richer and broader lists. That's one of the secrets of the audiences that you can build. Think about if you have prospects come in and they went through a few of the pages in the funnel, but then they didn't pull the trigger. Now they're in there for 180 days, since that's the max for most custom audiences (CAs). What we like to do is segment our CAs at 7 days, 14 days, 30 days, and up. As we scale, we get more people in the shorter time frame, and then that shorter time frame audience can be the basis of building a lookalike audience. If you have a lot of people at each step in a shorter time frame, generally they create really good lookalike audiences from the data because they are hot from the shorter time period. The more you scale, the more people are in there. That's how you can build these dynamic custom audiences, which then produce better results.

CURRENT TRENDS

The landscape has changed a great deal since Facebook started advertising. It was pretty clunky and awful in the beginning. Now, AI is really starting to come into its own. Facebook is really trying to optimize to make it easier for advertisers. That's where I see the landscape changing. If the algorithm--the optimization--continues to work in the right way, then it will make it easier to a degree. The one fundamental thing that people still have to understand, which they clearly don't, is that this is a great advertising platform. They're all great advertising platforms, but really, it's not about the platform. It's about zoning in with the right marketing message to the right people at the right time. You have to have the right offer in there, too, so it all makes sense to the audience that you are after.

I think the fundamentals of marketing are still the same, as people are still people. Platforms change, but people don't. Psychology hasn't changed, behavior hasn't changed, buyer intent hasn't changed, and the objections that you have to overcome haven't changed. I think people do, unfortunately, think Facebook will be easy. I think it will get easier, but you still need to be able to feed the machine. You still need to understand how you get inside someone's head or, more importantly, inside the conversation that's going on in their head. That's how you really get your marketing message to resonate. That's a fundamental you can't get away from, whether it's Instagram, Facebook, Twitter, Google, or YouTube. They're all brilliant platforms but you still can't lose the fundamentals of good old-fashioned direct response marketing.

At the end of the day, people don't just buy one thing. They buy hundreds of different products. What you need to do is find out what products are in demand for a mass market, and then understand the marketing message to get into the conversation that's already going on in their heads. Your marketing then has to attract and repel people, then make the offer. In that capacity, AI will be good for optimizing. In order to get it to work, though, you have to do a really good job with your marketing.

In terms of adapting, the biggest thing is understanding the whole customer experience and the behavioral life cycle. Big companies understand that the most expensive thing to do is acquire a new customer. A lot of smaller, younger companies get fixated on acquiring new customers. They forget their current customers and the post-purchase aspect. You really need to track and measure, or there's no way you're going to know what you can change to optimize the whole sales cycle.

You have to be looking at customer lifetime value versus what the real cost is, meaning the acquisition cost, what you make over a customer's lifetime, and what the latency of that period is. It's 5 times easier to get a customer to re-buy than to acquire new customers. You also need to understand your retention and your return rate. If you can track all of that, you can understand exactly how much your customers are worth. Once you understand that, you now have money and budget planned accurately to acquire even more customers. That's how you scale, but you can only scale if you know that process and what a customer is really worth. You have to know what you can afford. When it comes to affording to scale on traffic, whoever can pay the most to acquire the customer will win. When you know your numbers, you can identify this.

(This is why you need to read the bonus chapter at the end with Scott Desgrosseilliers of Wicked Reports.)

Anyone starting out is going to have a limited budget. If they're selling something that's cheap, they understand what their profit margin is. They understand that they're looking at a one-off sale. If a product costs $20 to produce and you sell it for $50, that's a margin of $30 profit. But what if acquiring a customer costs $35? That's a $5 loss. For anyone just starting out, this can look like a huge upset. They shut things off early because they don't have the budget yet. They don't yet have data to support what the customer lifetime value is.

A true calculation of customer lifetime value is 2 years of data. Anyone starting out doesn't have 2 years of data, of course. The only other thing you can look at before you look at lifetime values is the average cart value, or AOV. Generally, there isn't a traffic problem if you understand marketing and getting the right offer in front of people. The problem is that people get discouraged early when advertising costs are a little too high in relation to the actual front-end sales.

WHAT THE FUTURE HOLDS

I'm sure that AI will come into it. The future will likely see big new advertisers or big brands spending more money because they know that they've got the data to support testing it more. We're also likely to see the bigger advertisers spending even more money and getting a better return. I think it's the little guys without huge budgets who will have a hard time. The name of the game with paid advertising is paying to get data. You have to be prepared to spend a decent amount to get the data before you can interpret it and make informed decisions. As much as AI will help a majority of people, bigger brands and people with deeper pockets will see a bigger return.

In terms of the platform, they're going to continue to come out with different types of advertising. I think we're going to see a big continuation of video, live streaming, and live TV coming into its own as well. Those channels will be even better to market on, whereas TV advertising can't compete. The cost of getting in front of an audience that's now overwhelmingly on mobile devices is too cheap for TV to compete.

EFFECTIVE STRATEGIES

The biggest one for us is split testing new creatives and new audiences. When we start out, we're testing creatives. We're predominantly testing images and video. For example, we test 3 different audiences. That means 3 different ad sets and 1 target audience per ad set. We put 3 ads in each of those ad sets, to see which of those ad creatives resonates the most with the audiences. You can see what resonates when you look at the data. From there, we establish that we've got 1 or 2 winners. We can see which of those 3 audiences did the best with those creatives. Once we've done that, we start again. What we're really doing is looking at our target audience data because we want to understand who we're really trying to target.

Whether the creative engages the audience first is just as important. Engagement is key. It's all about stopping the scroll. Did it draw them in? Did we get that initial engagement and get their interest? The interest comes from the click. As you're looking at the data, you're really asking what creative resonated and got the click from the target audience. We use the 80/20 rule. On a campaign that is working, we're trying to spend 80% of our time or budget on things that work. We spend the other 20% on continual testing. We're always trying to beat the control, and that's a continuous process. You have to remember that this is an auction system.

All of the online paid advertising networks are auction systems. Every day is a different auction with different advertisers and budgets.

A result of understanding all of this is knowing when to cut things off early, but also when to let them go longer. This is the biggest problem we find with inexperienced advertisers. They don't know how to interpret the data and they get overwhelmed. You have to understand your end-to-end metrics. Otherwise, how can you optimize? How can you know what did or didn't work? If it did work, how can you know what return you got? If you understand the return, you can use the 80/20 rule with your budget.

When it comes to metrics, there are those on Facebook and those off Facebook. You can't control the metrics that are on Facebook. They're under Facebook's control. But you can control the metrics when they're on your site. A good example of that would be video views and engagement. The video is on Facebook, where people are engaging with it. They might watch 50% or so. That's a metric you really need to understand, in terms of engagement. Engagement is what gets you cheaper CPM. You're really looking to get the click. Nothing is going to happen until you get them somewhere to see an offer. However, we don't look at normal clicks, which could be someone clicking the video or image. We look at outbound clicks. An outbound click means they're going to the web page that we want to take them to from the ad. They've left Facebook, and now they're enroute to a totally different domain. It's your real estate. When they land on that real estate, you're in control of the metrics. Your advertising has done its job and Facebook is no longer in control.

Let's say they're on your landing page. That's a page view. So you fire that standard pixel, and they go to a product page and you get a content view. Now that they're looking at the information, you have to presale them. You have to determine if they're really interested. You have to repel and attract. From there, you can see the percentage of conversion. So if you do Facebook reports, you can now plan out the conversion rate from step 1 to step 2. From a content view, they could potentially push the button, whether it's Add to Cart or any other button. They're going deeper in the funnel. That tells you that they've gone from initial awareness to interest, and now they're giving you "behavioral type of interest."

So once they get to the cart page, the next step is deeper in the funnel, like initiating checkout. This whole time, you're learning more and more information. The important thing to look at, based on your campaign and targeting, is the conversion element at each point. That's important to record. If you had another ad set, you can then compare how far the audience went. It can also tell you if one is cheaper, but another one got you further through the funnel to purchase, for example.

Once you understand that process and what the conversion rate is, you can figure out how many sales, Initiate Checkouts, Add to Carts, and content views a campaign has. You can analyze this data and determine which campaign will have a higher ROI. Then, you put 80% of your budget on the one that's producing better results.

It's fundamental to your success. If you work out your numbers, you have an offer, you know how much it makes, you know how much the advertising costs, then you can look back up the funnel even before you start getting sales and know how many Add to Carts add up to a sale. This comes down to knowing your Add to Cart to checkout conversion rate, while tying that back into your advertising. If you know these numbers at each point, you know what your acceptable metrics are, whereas other people might get overwhelmed if the numbers don't look perfect and shut it down.

You're paying for the data until you can see that and make informed decisions. Informed decisions come in 2 forms. If it's not working, switch it off. If it is working, scale it. That's where you get to once you have enough data. It can take potentially 2,000 to 5,000 impressions depending on how many campaigns you have to get that data. Just keep in mind that if you don't interpret the data, you're never going to succeed with paid advertising.

CHAPTER 12

Enrico Lugnan: A Cutting-Edge Innovator

I'm a 25-year-old Italian guy who loves strategy. I'm the co-founder and CSO at Avenik, which is a social media marketing agency that helps brands and corporations to craft and execute their social media marketing and sales strategies. We started using social media around 2 years ago. We've gone into the strategic part after having grown a network from 0 to 8 million within a year. We've been helping companies craft and execute strategies for the past 12 months.

DIVING INTO FACEBOOK

We realized that a lot of businesses were really attached to the way they used to do marketing and only used social media marketing in a limited way. They only used basic ad campaigns, without going in-depth. From what I noticed, businesses seemed to be used to doing advertising more passively. For example, I noticed that businesses would be advertising passively rather than being more proactive in trying to actually find and create content that is designed to attract their targeted audience. At first, we assumed that a lot of companies already knew how to do that. After consulting with them, we realized that the strategic part of actually coming up with a campaign and how to structure it was a big pain point for a lot of companies.

Most companies see me talking about Instagram and Facebook in conjunction with each other because they are 2 sides of the same coin. We use Instagram for marketing and Facebook ads for sales. Being able to do this means we can test out the content and see how the audience reacts to the content on Instagram. We can test what type of audience and what type of pages actually give the best results. Facebook tracks all the custom events and custom conversions that happen in your marketing. With all of the targeting options you have on Facebook, you're able to retarget almost exactly who you want to based on actions and behaviors. In the past, there were a lot of companies that relied on detailed, narrow targeting on Facebook. If they were a sports company they looked for sports people and assumed it would work. Then they would use creatives that looked like they were from 1997. They would see campaigns fail and conclude that their product was not for Facebook ads. In reality, the creative and the targeting were most likely the problem. If you don't have perfect ad creatives but you have really good laser targeting, you can still reach your targeted audience. You can still have a positive ROI on Facebook pretty easily.

USEFUL TIPS

For clients that want to use Facebook and Instagram ads for their eCommerce businesses, they want us to help them find out the retargeting method they should use, how to optimize their content, or they want us to create an Instagram account to sell products for them. We tell them that the first thing they need to do is to actually not sell. You have to build up trust and an ad stack strategy first. The ROI for the first 30 days might be good. You might make $100,000 in 30 days with an eCommerce store selling something trending. That happens, but it's more likely to be the sort of thing that only works for 24 months. We try to build an infrastructure where they have a constant flow of targeted traffic. This is based on the constant flow and the behavior of the targeted traffic. It's also based on gender, device, frequency, average time on website, and all the parameters you can actually find out with analytics tools. We then proactively use the data to reach out to more targeted cold traffic. This level of analytics allows us to improve and expand results. We also always have an engagement campaign running that has nothing to do with sales whatsoever.

AN INSTAGRAM-FIRST APPROACH

As an example, a client sells interior design pieces. The regular approach would have been to focus on getting a positive ROI with a Facebook ads campaign just to show that in the first 60 days we can deliver a good ROI. This can lead to consistent growth when investing with a good budget, but he wanted to take a different route. This different route worked well for us and this client understood the need for long-term ROI rather than quick, short-term ROI. So, he allowed us to focus on building up his Instagram account. He respected us as experts and was all in on what we could do.

We started by putting together an Instagram account that reached around 11,000 followers in the first 2 months. Based on that, we knew what type of content worked best, what type of interior design images worked best, and especially what type of influencers worked best. I'm not talking about the overpriced verified accounts that sell bikinis and have over 200,000 followers. I'm talking about the 45-year-old housewife from Norway who really loves interior design. We talked to around 25 influencers of this kind and shipped products to them. We had some really great feedback from actual people in the industry. We realized that there were 4 or 5 items that everyone was choosing, and the remaining 14 weren't being chosen. So we shipped that handful of items. We took the user-generated content from the influencers and created a carousel campaign with the top 5 selling items. We generated a bit of traffic, populated the pixels, started retargeting a lookalike audience off of the audience that we had generated, and the job was done. Over a week, we got a consistent 980% ROI. In the first 48 hours after we launched on Instagram, we had around 380 clicks just from our Instagram profile.

INFLUENCER MARKETING

Before doing influencer marketing and paying an influencer, we always ship 20-50 products to 20-50 different influencers to gather the data. First of all, you get 20-50 pieces of content for free. You don't actually pay for the creative and they deliver good content. Second of all, if an influencer actually really likes the product, they might tag you more than once. I recommend being polite and sending back a discount code or something along those lines if that happens. You can try to start that kind of a relationship, but if you're not able to do that, you really need to rely on analytics. You don't have comprehensive analytics for Instagram, but you have access to the number of likes. You have access to the number of comments. You have access to the number of followers. You have websites like Social Blade that can tell you how the followers are growing or not growing. Then we put in some old stats, manually checking the last 20 posts' likes and comments, and the ratio. The math is in identifying the engagement rates, which can tell us which piece of content is performing better. When we identify which profiles are performing best, we deliver the products to them. For example, before finding our 25 influencers for the last campaign, we analyzed 300 accounts before identifying the 25 that we wanted to recruit into our campaign.

As far as contacting them, we don't reach out to them like an agency. We just reach out to them like a regular human being. We're not trying to start a business relationship. We just explain that we like their page and we have a product we think they might like if they're willing to give us a shout-out. It's very straightforward and casual. It's just a private message and an email. If they reply, they reply. If they don't, I move on. I have enough numbers, so I repeat the process for other profiles. This works for micro-influencers, too. Anyone below 100,000 followers, you can actually reach out to them and start something like this. If they have a really well-engaged audience, even an account with less than 10,000 followers can actually provide 10 sales with one shout out, as long as the product is aligned with their audience and makes sense for them to sell.

CURRENT TRENDS

I wouldn't say it's a trend yet, but I think Facebook chatbots with engagement ad campaigns and content marketing ad campaigns will become a trend. Not Facebook chatbots to sell, but simply Facebook chatbots to give customer support and act as a content marketing platform. I envision people using them to share real value, like an engaged newsletter done via chatbot. Even the open rates and click-through rates--based on actual engagement from a post, not a message campaign or a lead magnet campaign--are going to be something big. It won't be for everyone, but the ones who will adopt it will make good ROI.

ADAPTING

Companies need to realize that sales advertising is dying, and there is nothing they can do to stop it. That's just a shift of the market and the culture. In the 80s you had TV shows with advertisements that were really salesy on all the bad channels that no one watches. That's the shift that's happening on Facebook ads, too. That's why influencer marketing works. It never worked for Facebook because Facebook became overcrowded, noisy, and spammy as it aged. On Instagram, you're still able to find the right content from the right influencers because it's a content-based platform. Facebook is more like a comment-based platform, so the content isn't really king. On Instagram, content is king, and the same thing can happen on Facebook ads if you do the right retargeting and match the right ad with the right type of content.

I'm not trying to say that Instagram is the best platform, but I see that the real type of value is in the content. Right now, Instagram is the best content-driven platform. YouTube is also a content-driven platform, but also really crowded. It's really competitive and sometimes it can be harder to actually scroll through YouTube and find the content. The YouTube algorithm doesn't really help you to find the content you might be interested in. It's more about monetization ads and in-stream video ads, which you don't really have on Instagram. A really cool thing you find both on Facebook and Instagram is that the ads are exactly like posts. If I scroll through Instagram, I don't notice an ad. If I see an ad on Instagram Stories, it looks like an Instagram Story. It has to be 15 seconds, the same as any other Instagram Story. That's why I think the platform is growing. In order to be approved and in order to perform, you need to have good content.

WHAT TO AVOID

As Instagram grew over the last 6 months and as Facebook was booming, companies weren't really able to keep up organically, so they started faking it. They started buying fake followers first on Twitter, then on Facebook, now on Instagram. A real company with a real framework and a real long-term, good business model shouldn't rely on vanity metrics. They aren't important. What matters at the end of the month, depending on the business model you have, is the return on ad spend, customer acquisition costs, and customer lifetime value. The number of likes and followers aren't important. If you think that buying followers will help you, you don't really understand how the algorithm works. Avoid anything that's fake on a content-driven platform, because it's based on content and based on engagement.

ON CHATBOTS

The strategic advantage that a messenger chatbot can provide is the response time. If you know your target audience and your product, ideally you also know the top 5-15 questions anyone can have. Customer support is answering the same questions 95% of the time. Using the chatbot for engagement, rather than selling and trying to get them to the discount code or coupon, you help them. Of course, the first message when the customer reaches out can give them a chosen set of answers. 'What's the problem?' 'How can I help you?' 'Do you want to schedule a call?' You can integrate scheduling a call with the messenger bot.

If you know what ManyChat is and you know what Zapier is, you can basically do anything you want. You are able to collect emails, put them on a Google Sheet, and use Zapier to move them from your Google Sheet to your Marketing software, and then to your Calendly. You can have everything connected from booking to scheduling the call to creating the Zoom conference link. You automate it once they reach out to you. They click the right set of options and you have a call with them within 24 hours. Even the real companies that have real people doing this aren't really able to manage it effectively within 24 hours. A chatbot actually can.

(This is why you need to read the bonus chapter at the end with Karl Schuckert of Segmate.)

WHAT THE FUTURE HOLDS

The development of Facebook ads and its trends depend on how many users apply the best practices. For example, the latest update where Facebook is prohibiting the initial coin offerings (ICOs) or anything relating to cryptocurrency, it's because everyone overused it. We had people going with get rich quick schemes. We had fake ICOs. We had illegal white papers. Facebook cannot have legal problems that arise from people advertising the wrong way. So assuming that everyone uses the platform in the right way and assuming that Facebook is showing everyone that it wants to reduce spam, I see Facebook and social media remaining a content- and interaction-based platform. However, I think that the tools Facebook has will be a lot more about content. If you have a blog or a podcast and you don't have a Facebook ad strategy, you're losing out big time. Your podcast and your blog can sell for you depending on what you are selling. Distributing a blog and a podcast on Facebook with advertising is a good practice. If everyone uses the best practices, rather than trying to get rich quick, there's going to be a lot more valuable content.

You need to keep gathering data about your ideal customer. You have to keep understanding the customer more deeply. Once you're able to do that, you're also able to create the right content for that customer. If you have the right reach, just 10,000 impressions is all you need if they're all the right ones. If you actually target your content and you keep researching, don't stop. Don't assume you know enough. Try to go deeper and keep split testing. Ideally, it's not going to work in 2 weeks or 6 weeks, but 6 months from now, every ad you run is going to be 1000% ROI.

EFFECTIVE STRATEGIES

You have to put yourself in the right position to understand the data. You have to actually understand what it means. You have to understand why. If frequency goes up, your cost per click might go up. If you know where you want to go with this, so you're focusing on where you want to go 10 steps from now, you should be the first one to understand the data. A data analyst can understand the data for what it means in that spreadsheet, but they can't see the data within your bigger scheme.

Another important step is to understand the client, including the client's ego. We had a consulting call with a company that was selling high-end lingerie. They were complaining about the fact that a lot of the female influencers that we were using had predominantly male audiences, but they were trying to sell to a female audience because the end user was a female. We tried to make them understand that there are not a lot of women who like to see other women looking better than them in that type of outfit. You will still have a decent portion of the market that are women who love the product, but the impulsive buyer in that specific market is the guy who buys the product because he wants his girlfriend to look like the model. You need to understand these unique nuances in your market.

Of course, you might be wrong sometimes. Everyone will be wrong at some point. You might have made a wrong assumption that kept compounding as you grew what you thought was your ideal customer audience, throwing off all of your marketing. That's why you need to keep split testing and gathering data.

A couple of years back, companies understood that Facebook ads were an ocean. I had massive returns back then. Unfortunately, eCommerce stores now have to realize that Facebook ads are no longer an ocean, but they still can be profitable. Of the strategies we've used for clients, one is for pure Facebook sales. It's a pure Facebook content marketing funnel. You're starting a funnel based on engagement, retargeting based on people who engaged. You're also creating lookalike audiences from the engagement and refining this audience over time. You're trying to go from engagement to traffic, then from traffic to specific custom conversions based on your funnel. Just keep delivering the actual content and making sure that people can connect. If you are able to do that, they feel like they're connecting to you.

Another strategy that's worked really well is connecting micro-influencer marketing with Facebook ads. Micro-influencer marketing will help you generate the first type of traffic and the first reports of ad performance data. You can retarget this traffic with everything you have access to with Facebook ads. Another option is that you can use remarketing tools outside of Facebook that use the Facebook ad pixel too, like Adroll.

One thing that we work on with our biggest clients is helping them act as a media company. Try to imagine you are the main distributor of valuable content, whether it is blogs, podcasts, Instagram pages, Facebook pages, or a YouTube channel. You have to be the authority there. You're not a newspaper. There are no magazines that control the market anymore. Last year in the US, Facebook advertising total spend was around $20 billion. All advertising spend on print in the US was about the same. The problem is that anyone between 14-34 doesn't buy magazines anymore. This means that your brand can now become the modern day magazine that they consume. It can be costly, though. However, if you have the budget and the expertise to do it, that's a unicorn strategy that will separate you from your competition.

These strategies are based on the actual content and market. If the content changes and the market changes, you have to change. Micro-influencers that work now might not work 6 months from now. But as long as you keep split testing and gathering data to respond or evolve, I don't think these strategies will go anywhere in the next 24 months.

Discover how the ARM5 Formula has helped companies do $93,000 in one day (138,497% ROAS), $330,000 during Black Friday 2019 (6349% ROAS), $274,000 during Valentine's Day 2019 (1531% ROAS), and an average 1480.61% ROAS throughout 2019 by going to **www.joshmarsden.com/success**

CHAPTER 13

David Schloss: THE Facebook Advertising LEGEND

In 2007, I started online marketing from my apartment. I first got introduced to it through affiliate marketing and SEO, and I fell in love with paid ads as time went on. After 1 or 2 years, it really started to kick in that paid ads were where I would be able to deliver on being a data lover. I love numbers. I'm someone who can analyze when things are about to take off or if they're not quite there yet. Being a mathematical mind, paid ads seemed to be the easiest marketing form to focus on. It was literally automatic. I knew what to do there.

I've been doing paid ads for about 12 years now, and I've had the agency for the last 10, focusing on Facebook and Instagram ads. My agency has gone through its trials and tribulations. It's gone through multiple iterations of what it needs to be. We'll spend anywhere between $2 million to $3 million a month in a given time span. Over the holidays, you can double or triple that.

FUNDAMENTAL DIFFERENCES BETWEEN FACEBOOK AND INSTAGRAM

Instagram and Facebook are nearly identical in nature. Someone who's viewing a piece of content on Instagram is pretty much the same person on

Facebook. The intent of the user is almost the same now compared to last year, when everything was more of an impulse on Instagram. You still can get that behavior on Facebook--that's always been there--but a Facebook user typically takes a little longer to make a decision. You have more time to convince them or persuade them. You have longer-form content on Facebook. On Instagram, 60 seconds is the cutoff.

Now, Instagram TV is still relatively new. The ability to advertise with a long-form piece of content on IGTV is still up in the air. Some people say it will happen, but some say it won't. They keep playing with it. Sometimes it's available, but sometimes it's not. It's in beta constantly. Facebook wants to create their own little YouTube, and they're doing it natively within Instagram. They know that a lot of these users on Instagram stay there and keep scrolling. It's the same behavior as Facebook, except it's a much quicker scroll. Instagram lets you go through a lot of content faster.

Instagram gives you 15 seconds with stories and 30-60 seconds with videos. If people put up images that don't grab someone's attention, the audience keeps scrolling. With the introduction of IGTV, they want to recreate that long-form experience that was already created on Facebook. However, the older generation keeps getting older on Facebook.

Nearly everyone has a Facebook account at this point. They may not even be using it if they only have one in order to get on Instagram. So there's this dynamic around the intent of being on either platform. Am I connecting with people on a deeper level? I would use Facebook. Am I just in the mood to scroll, learn, even be introduced to new people? I would use Instagram.

Only some people have been given the ability to test out ads on IGTV. IGTV works to promote an ad, and then it shows up on the Instagram Explore page. It doesn't necessarily show up as sponsored in the feed. But if you can boost it, then it shows up on Instagram Explore. Now for those of you who are actively advertising, you should see that the Instagram Explore page is an option. You can manufacture virality. Before, you could only get on the Instagram Explore page if either you were near somebody influential or your stuff was getting shared a lot. Now you can just put a few dollars behind it and you're at the top, or at least somewhere in the middle of the page. People don't even know it's sponsored.

When it comes to IGTV, I can't select my post to boost it as an advertisement. I can't use a post ID like I can with Facebook ads. It either shows up or it doesn't through organic reach. Most of the time, it doesn't get much reach. Therefore, you don't really get the option of promoting your long-form content on IGTV. Normally, you just have to cut it into pieces and hope that's enough to be able to turn it into something that gets traction on IGTV.

It used to be that, in order for you to watch it, you had to move over to the other side of a profile where all the IGTV stuff was. You had to go find it, or you had to click a button for it to open up IGTV. Now it's simultaneous. When you click the button, it populates on your phone. It's easy. When you tried that before, it would just show a blank screen. It wasn't working correctly. There were so many bugs with IGTV. I think the way that they've integrated it into the feed now and how the feed is actively used, is why more and more people are using IGTV. Now you see YouTube videos or long-form Facebook videos that people are just uploading directly to IGTV. When it was first introduced, no one was really up to the idea of stopping everything to watch a 3-minute video, but now they're noticing that people are now watching it all the way through.

The users of IGTV get a lot of preferential treatment. It used to be that if you frequently posted on Facebook, you were always at the top of the feed. You were getting a lot of organic reach. People were interacting with your posts because you were the most active. If the people who were engaging with you continued to engage, you stayed at the top of the feed. Now with Instagram, it seems that if you use IGTV often and people engage with that content, you always appear at the top.

Now consider the fact that the sizing of the video content is different. Even when you create something on another platform, you can't just upload it. You have to finesse the dimensions or videos get stretched too tall or too wide. I think that contributes to why not many people use it. It's a little thing, but a novice isn't going to want to have to reproduce their content.

Content has always been a priority. We've always known it's a priority. Now consider the introduction of all these new platforms. All these different platforms work best with different dimensions and different lengths. Certain content performs better on different platforms. There's no way you could utilize all of them yourself. Furthermore, if you're an eCommerce store with 20 products, how are you going to edit content for each product across each platform with just 1 or 2 computers? On top of that, you have to record, get a microphone, get the video, get the stand, and make sure everything's perfect. It's too much for someone to handle alone.

Either you have to designate an entire day to content creation and keep it in-house, or you pay someone to help you out. At the end of the day, knowing how much you're out there for people to trust is going to become incredibly important. It's always been important, but now it seems to be that even scammers are great at content production. They can hire a video person, just like you can. They can set everything up to look like a great person. That doesn't mean they are. So if you want to stand out and be the 5-star provider in your space, you want to have the best products out there with the best showcase. You have to put the time and effort into the content. You have to be able to reproduce it at scale on all these different platforms over time.

WHAT WORKS

We used to have everything set to ad budget optimization (ABO) vs. campaign budget optimization (CBO). It's funny, considering CBO is another feature of Facebook Advertising that's fairly new. When CBO first came out, it wasn't something that was used effectively. A lot of the results we were getting were terrible. It just wasn't ready yet.

Now, it's the default. Not for every account, but that will likely change. As of right now, most accounts are starting to transition, so a lot of our processes revolve around using CBO compared to what they were with ABO.

We used to do every ad set. Every interest would have its own dedicated ad set. You would set them all to a specific budget and run them all. You might put 3 creatives in each of the ad sets. In our case, it would be 3 different videos with the same copy, or the same video with 3 different pieces of copy. You would let the interests run, take the best performers, scale them, and bundle them together. CBO disrupted that flow. Now, everything's done on the campaign level. If you put a minimum and maximum spend, there's no guarantee that all of the ad sets are going to bring in the numbers you want each day unless you set your campaign budget to a very high amount.

You're leaving everything to Facebook. Based on your optimization, whether you're trying to get leads, purchases, or Add to Carts, the budget will favor whichever one is getting the most of that specific set optimization goal. If it's purchases, that may not sound like a big deal; you want the most purchases anyway. However, you will have days where the ad set does not produce sales, and yet $500 was spent on that ad set. You've lost a lot of money. It doesn't always shift to a better performer, as it takes the whole lifetime of the ad campaign into account.

At some point, though, I'm sure this will be almost foolproof. What will end up being the hardest part is determining what audience to target, if you're funnel is converting, or if your ad is getting any attention. That will be the new sets of core focuses. Ads management will no longer be about turning things on and off.

For now, though, it's still up to us as the ad managers to determine whether or not an audience is going to produce what we want it to produce. The machine doesn't quite see it on a day-by-day basis. It just sees if there's sales consistency and it keeps spending. Facebook's machine learning with CBO hasn't reached its full potential yet. Now, our strategy is utilizing what's called a 4x2 or a 4x3. The 4 is the amount of ad sets in a campaign. The additional number is the amount of creative running within each ad set.

We'll do 3 if we're looking to test 3 videos, 3 pieces of copy, 3 different images, or a variation of that. We'll do 2 if we're focused on our best performers. I say 2 because you end up having at least 2 best performers from all your previous tests. Sometimes you'll have more, but you're generally good with 2. There's always something that's the same about them. A video might be the same but with different copy in 2 ads, and so on. If we want to target 1 interest at a time, we have 1 campaign at a time. Ten interests will take 10 campaigns. It's not fun, but you have to do it. We'll start with what we call the template ad set, where we set up everything. This is with the first interest that we're targeting.

Let's just say I'm targeting fans of Shark Tank. So, I start a campaign and target Shark Tank. I set all the options up in the campaign and ad set, and then I put my 3 ads in there. Let's say I want to test 3 different videos with the same copy. We take that ad set, and we duplicate it 4 more times, so it's a 4x3. We set it to publish, and we repeat that for every interest we want to target. Facebook will have days where all 4 ad sets are producing sales, and then they'll have days where only 2 of them are. On those days, you just turn off the other 2. You'll probably have no idea why it varies so much. It's the same audience and the same ads. All you're doing is turning off what's not producing for you. It doesn't always make sense, but it's best to just let it go.

You allow Facebook to determine which of the ads are working within that segment. When an ad is delivered in that one ad set, even though it's all the same interest, this group in ad set 1 is very different from ad set 2. If the audience is a million people, each ad set is pulling a different group that day. Every now and again, there will be overlap, but most of the time, they're pulling different segments, especially if your ad budget is at $300 a day or less. We can do this at scale. Imagine if you have lookalikes, interest groups, and so on. Imagine how many times you could duplicate this. It's hard to say how long this will work, though. Every year, we have to retool our strategy again.

Even with the old ad set optimization format, it was always set to pick the target. The evolution of that was to pick a target and advertise on mobile vs. desktop. Then it would evolve again with the option to do more than mobile and desktop. It would evolve placement-wise, or the audience would evolve. There are all sorts of ways you can finesse it and optimize for specific options.

You could still do those things, but you have to organize it all starting at the campaign level instead of the previous ad set level. The strategy itself is the same in terms of how you could segment, but it's a lot of duplication. I used to have campaigns where I could run 100 ad sets and it would be no problem. Now if you do that, it would barely spend unless you set the budget on the campaign level to thousands of dollars per day. It wouldn't make sense. Now, it's all become micromanagement.

I'm doing things more methodically now. A lot of clients don't want to see 30 campaigns go out in a day, and 20 of them may have to be turned off. What they'd prefer to see is the stacking of winners over time. I like to take things that work and progressively move up the chain until I have a group of ads that are consistently producing at the return on ad spend we want to see. Let's say I do 5-10 audience tests per day. While I'm doing those tests, I still have winners running. Those winners are making up for the losses that we're incurring because of those newer ad sets that aren't producing. They are all evening each other out for at least a week. For the rest of the month, we're scaling the winners. Unfortunately, that's the way we have had to do things. A lot of clients don't like that. Then, all of a sudden, they forget about it. They forget it even happened because of the results.

We do weekly and monthly analyses, not daily. But we have to get our testing done, or else we can't improve things. We'd rather get it all out of the way early, so then we can scale the rest of the month. These scalable campaign assets run for 6 months sometimes, and we just keep going. You just have to keep finding more audiences and trying to scale.

Now, on the Instagram side of things, we've gone very heavy with Stories. Last year, I did 12 case studies in 12 days with a Christmas theme.

I posted a case study on Instagram Stories because we were still actively running it with one of my clients at the time. They had their biggest months back to back using Instagram Stories for Black Friday and Cyber

Monday promotions. It started at Thanksgiving and we were running it into Christmas. In 2 months, they made something like $600,000, and they had never done that before. In December, we ended up doing about $580,000, so we practically doubled in a month. We were only using Stories!.

The reason why is because we found that demographics of 18-30, if you can show them the right message with a cheap product and continue to market to them to make them want something badly enough, they will spend a lot of money. Especially during a time where everyone assumes that everything is on discount. When we're doing a product launch, we like to launch during a time when people are already buying things. Even though ad costs were slightly higher, we barely noticed because our CPAs were low. For a product that we were selling for $50, we were getting a CPA of $15. We were still making a pretty good amount of money by the time it was shipped out.

We were selling close to 1,000 units a day sometimes. We were ecstatic to see that. We had never gone all-in with Instagram Stories before. Back in the holiday season of 2018, it was just 15 seconds. Now you can do 3 sets of 15 seconds, so it can be a 45-second video. It's progressive. We find those do really well for demonstration videos. The product that we were selling at the time required a demonstration. It was a phone accessory. I have to show how it works or else you're not going to buy it. It did so well when that was introduced because it was introduced at the top of 2018 during the hot buying season and we were able to keep promoting it deep into 2019. The extended Instagram Stories actually prolonged the life span of the promotion. We were able to run the same ads without the Black Friday and Cyber Monday tagging on it, just like the base ads. We were able to continue to run those all the way until mid-February of 2019 because people were still interested and we were staying in front of them.

We found that Stories work really well for the young demographic. This isn't surprising, but you have to be able to grab their attention quickly.

You can create so many variations. At that time, we were testing anywhere between 20-25 variations of sometimes 2 different videos. There were subtle differences in each one. Sometimes it was a different actor or a different shirt. We really mixed it up. We tried different things for the sake of it and some started to work. There was a period where we had 8-10 variations of each actor we were using. Even running 10 different ads for this person, they're all working. We were finding tons of success with Instagram Stories.

From a Facebook perspective, the feed is still great. We still use 60-second videos or shorter. What I love is the fact that I still have the ability to retarget based on the video views. They've also added in the ability to do the video views from Instagram. Last year, that was Facebook only. Now you can also do video audiences from Instagram. We've become very creative with that, especially considering if people are watching 50% of your 30-second video. Eventually that builds to watching a whole Story.

We started getting really creative with the retargeting aspect. If you saw something on the feed, we were going to retarget you with a Story. We kept doing things like that. As you can tell, we love Instagram. It sells a ton for eCommerce companies. However, if you have something that's perceived as a low-quality product, you have to prepare for an ever-growing amount of comments about how terrible the video is. You can have a mess when it comes to comments on Instagram. Of course, it could be the same way on Facebook. If your ad is not hitting the nail on the head, it can go viral in a negative way very quickly. You have to be careful.

Instagram is also integrating shopping features. You can tag your product and the price point. I wouldn't say that everyone has it, though. It's still being rolled out to everyone on the platform.

Then you have things like carousel ads. You had carousels in the past, but it wasn't as good as it is now. Now it's clean and it works well. It doesn't cause any crashing on the phone app. They're just adding more features, like tagging multiple products in the image. That's going to make it very easy for people with Shopify stores or any other platform. Before, the audience had to swipe up or click the button or else they wouldn't see the product. Now, there are multiple ways for you to showcase it.

Instagram shares similarities with Facebook. Facebook is integrating all of these features on Instagram because they know that people like us are there. We're browsing and searching the Instagram Explore page. It has a section for shopping and I go there just to look at what gadgets are being sold. If something is on the Instagram Explore page, that means that there are a lot of people engaging with it. The Instagram Explore page automatically puts you in the mood to buy, but that's the great thing about it.

You know what they're doing. Plus with IGTV, if you do demonstration videos, you could sell that. Imagine what happens when you do the long-form video on IGTV on a deeper level, where people who are following your page are now able to see the full demonstration of how the product works. You couldn't do this before on Instagram. You used to have to go to Google. Now they're putting all of that on the app.

WHAT THE FUTURE HOLDS

It's not just Facebook Ads that people are talking about now. Facebook Ads are still very easy for people to jump on and start, but you should've already been on the ad platform by now. You should've already been doing something because it's just getting tougher by the day. You're going to be competing against people who have been advertising and are tenured professionals. Bottom line, if you want to be able to sell, get active. Start creating your ad creatives. Start practicing using the ad platform itself by deploying some ads. Start putting the work in now.

Trend-wise, I'm seeing more people focusing on Instagram ads. That's very obvious. If you want to sell something to a younger demographic, they're all on Instagram. If you want to sell something to an older generation, they're on Facebook primarily. There's an age demographic where it's split. I get targeted on both because I'm 31. Once you hit around the age of 40, you start to notice you don't get targeted much on Instagram. If you are, it's not even with offers that you would typically look into. With eCommerce stores, you can target everybody, depending on what you're selling. A phone accessory, for example, is for everybody. Do you have a phone specific to this product? You could potentially buy it from an Instagram or Facebook ad. However, if we're talking about golf clubs, you're not going to get shown an ad if you're under the age of 40. The majority of golf club sales come from people 50 and over. Most of those ads are going to show up on Facebook because that's where the older demographic is residing.

The demographic split is becoming a lot more obvious. Depending on your market and how you're marketing, that will determine which platform you use the most. For example, some of my clients want to generate applications online. They want people to fill in information on a form and get on the phone. If you try that on Instagram, it's highly unlikely anyone will take time away from a 60-second video to go fill out a form that takes them 3 minutes. However, if they're also present on Facebook, there's a higher probability of them filling out an application on Facebook. It's as if being on Facebook flips a switch, and they realize they're interacting with actual people.

How you present yourself on the platform will determine how exactly you consume it, whether it's filling out a form or purchasing something. One of my team members once called it branded consumption. On Instagram, for example, we have to keep everything short. We have no choice. How do you brand your application if you're trying to get someone to apply for something or buy something and have them do it as quickly as possible? If they're consuming in 60 seconds, wouldn't it be great to purchase something in 60 seconds, too?

Imagine reducing your purchase process to a couple of clicks and you're done. If I'm on Instagram, I'm doing things quickly. If you can keep it in that same light, you're going to get a lot more sales. But you're also going to get a lot more headaches in the beginning. Some people are going to say they didn't even know they bought something. You have to basically teach people how the process works through consuming something on Instagram. We have some buy pages we're only getting traffic to from

Instagram. We would use a custom page, directing people where to click if they want to buy the product or a bundle. But what ends up happening is, when you select one of these options, there are only a couple things left you have to do. You have to fill in the shipping and payment details, of course, but after you do that, it's all on the same page. You fill it in, click submit, and it's done in 2 clicks.

On the regular store site, though, you have to go to the checkout, initiate the checkout, fill in details, go to the shipping page, and then you're done. On your desktop or laptop, that's fine. On the desktop, people want to go through that process. They want a pop-up for an extra 10% off. They want something saying they'll get another 15% off if they try to abandon the cart. People know how this works. We're creating our process to fit the person's interaction speed and how they're consuming.

With Facebook, you can do multiple steps. You can offer discounts. You can do all the extra steps for conversion, in the event of someone seeing it on mobile and wanting to save it for when they're at a desktop. Not everyone wants to buy something on their phone. Imagine if you're doing that to someone who's 50 years old. Do you really think they want to buy on mobile? Most of them don't even want to use a phone.

We're focusing more on the length of the purchase and how quickly it can be done. The ads work exactly the same. It's just getting tougher. Your creative needs to stand out or you're not going to get sales. It's all about making sure that you can shorten the buying process. You need to be in front of the right people on the right platform, and you need to cut out anything that doesn't seem to be worthwhile in the interest to checkout path. We're barely running desktop traffic anymore. It's all mobile. Facebook tells you to run automatic placements. Most of your traffic is still mobile. Even when you put everything on automatic, it's primarily mobile.

Now it's more about condensing the purchase process and creating ads that are grabbing attention. The more attention it grabs, the cheaper your cost becomes from a CPM level and click-cost level, which leads to a cheaper cost to acquire a customer. You let the creative pinpoint the people who actually want to buy the product.

I used to have ugly ads. I would use stock photos with crazy borders to grab attention, and they would work. But people have gotten smarter now. If they want to buy something from you, especially in the eCommerce world, you have to showcase your product. At the end of the day, they want to know what they're buying before they buy it. You have to put a lot more effort into selling something than even 2 years ago.

EFFECTIVE STRATEGIES

If you have a store of multiple products, this is helpful. There are dynamic catalog ads that you can put together with 3 or 4 clicks. They pull images from your store and create ads for you based on the last product that someone visited. They work like a charm. They are typically the highest-performing return-on-ad-spend, profitable ads that we run in an eCommerce store. One day, there may not be any sales. The next day, you have 9 sales that come in just from that ad. It's dynamically done based on someone's intent, so it's very easy to set up. I typically do it based on time increments, meaning the last 7, 14, 30, and 60 days they've been on the store. At each level, we incorporate a different discount. By the time they buy, they get excluded, and they no longer see it anymore. The hope is that they buy within the 7-day period, which most people do. You show them a 5%-10% discount and they're good.

Once you make it beyond that point, when they get to the 14-day period, you might increase the discount by 5%. Be aware of your margins, though. Try to keep the CPA low. That's the whole point of using this campaign. Even if you throw in a discount, you have to keep your cost per acquisition low anyway. By the time they get to that 30-day period, they're at the max discount that you'll give away.

If they make it past 60 days, they weren't going to buy anyway. The whole goal is that you're trying to get them to buy immediately with the smallest discount. What will likely happen is that you'll end up finding that a lot of people tend to buy during the 7-day period and 14-day period. On that same note, you can use this same setup with people who viewed a specific product or collection, or even people who made it to the cart but never finished their purchase. These types of ads will still dynamically pull the last thing that they saw. You can put the discount code in the copy. This works for us every time.

Another thing you need to do is run ads thanking customers when they've bought something for the first time or recently. We retarget our customers and say, "Thank you so much for buying. As a token of appreciation, here's an extra 15% off of your next order." That runs for 3 days. It's only for purchasers. You would be surprised how many people come back and decide they might as well buy something else if they have 15% off. It's like fan appreciation or customer appreciation. That same notion could be done through email, so we implement it with email and an ad.

Finally, if you have a product that you can demonstrate, the 45-second Instagram Story broken into 3 15-second pieces works incredibly well. Another way that you can use them is to showcase up to 3 different products in a story, with each product getting 15 seconds. For us, the page that they land on has all 3 products on the page, set up so they can buy them individually or as a bundle. Especially during the holidays, this would be a great idea to test it as a holiday bundle.

They're all complementary. Phone accessories are a good example. Here are the phone accessories that you could bundle together: a phone charging case, a wireless charger that you could put your phone on top of, a car charger, and then a bonus item that would probably work with a secondary device. All 4 of those things go together.

Our landing page is a custom sales page. If you're using Shopify, you can use Zipify or something like that to create a custom page. At the very top of the page, we would typically put the same video we just put on Instagram Stories, but the longer version. No jump cuts, just 45-seconds through.

On the right side, we'll put something to direct attention below, because we have the 4 boxes below the video. We're giving you the chance to buy into our holiday bundle. You can get each one of these for 10% off, or you can get the whole holiday bundle for 23% off. If they choose the holiday bundle, it's hundreds of dollars vs. if they choose 1 product. We try to position it so it doesn't make sense for you to buy 1 item because you're only getting a small percentage off. We want you to buy the holiday bundle. You get a larger percentage off, but what people don't realize is we're using the same ad. A lot of people end up taking that $150 bundle for the same CPA we were getting when we were selling a single $50 product. This works out for different holidays throughout the year. It all depends on what you're selling.

Discover how the ARM5 Formula has helped companies do $93,000 in one day (138,497% ROAS), $330,000 during Black Friday 2019 (6349% ROAS), $274,000 during Valentine's Day 2019 (1531% ROAS), and an average 1480.61% ROAS throughout 2019 by going to www.joshmarsden.com/success

CHAPTER 14

Cody Neer: The Best of the Best in E-Commerce Advertising

I grew up in Central Florida with a heavy sports background. I was a baseball player. I even went to the University of Florida to play baseball. I came out of school and went straight into professional baseball. I realized that pro baseball was a short-lived career a few years in, so when I got out of that I was looking for the next step. That's when I jumped into entrepreneurship and digital marketing. I founded an electronic check payment processing company. I knew nothing about the industry. I was just a salesman at the time, but I learned a lot about it. Several years into that business, we had to generate our own leads and find our own customers. The whole journey of making stuff happen led me into the Facebook advertising digital marketing world. The experiences from that business took me into a role at Target Corporation in Minneapolis, where we led their first Facebook ads. There were 5 global companies, with Target being one of them, and we were one of the first anywhere to run a Facebook ad. We had a golden opportunity with nearly an unlimited budget with a brand like Target and that's where I got my feet wet in eCommerce.

From there I started my own brands in eCommerce. That's the first domino that spurred me on to decide I could run ads and sell my own products via Facebook ads. Fast forward to today and that's where I am.

FUNDAMENTAL DIFFERENCES BETWEEN FACEBOOK AND INSTAGRAM ADS

Instagram is very visual. It's not a data feed, so when you're looking at Instagram everything has to be visually appealing. It has to grab attention. That's why you constantly see fitness models in their bathing suits or yoga pants getting the most attention and eyeballs. Facebook is one and the same on what's successful. You need to be visually appealing with videos and images. However, Facebook is more about engagement than Instagram.

WHAT'S WORKING

Video ads are serving us well on Facebook. I can take a customer through a journey of what the product is, who you are, how it's going to help, and so on and so forth. That's typically what drives the most results for us on Facebook ads. We have what they call a Facebook funnel. We're obviously going to drive cold traffic to our product, brand, or store. Then we're going to create audiences based on the actions they take inside that funnel.

For example, let's take someone who's never seen the product, never heard of us, and never done any kind of transaction with us. We're going to run a video that's going to catch their attention and get them to see who we are and why they should like us. We want them to understand our name and our brand. Then we're going to take someone who's viewed that, clicked on it, gone to the store, maybe added a product to the cart, and even purchased from us. Those are going to be the handful of different actions that they could take. Then we're going to create lookalikes and we're going to tell Facebook to find people who look just like these people that have taken these actions. Then we're going to run a similar video ad to those lookalike audiences that are going down the next step of the funnel. The final step would involve people who bought something, which is going to be the closest aligned to the people who you want to run ads to. We're going to create those similar lookalikes and run another video ad that's different than the first and second ads. It's going to be based on edutainment--that's education plus entertainment--or a testimonial on the product. We run them through those 3 sets of video series until they become a buyer. Obviously, once you become a buyer, you get a totally different set of video ads or marketing from us.

On Instagram, if I'm selling a physical product, I'll use an eye-catching picture of a model with our product; mock-ups and still images of just the product itself don't perform as well. If we can show an actual human being and humanize the product with someone interacting with it, that seems to give us the best result with Instagram ads. We will also leverage our testimonials through Instagram. That will be where we show an actual end user using or interacting with the product. That's a great touchpoint in the middle of the actual funnel on Instagram. User-generated content on Instagram in the middle of the funnel seems to be our best bet.

We have an order system that's 100% automated. Once we know the order is fulfilled, we have an average ship time. Once we see that the actual order has been delivered, then our first email goes out and asks if there was anything wrong with the product. If they report back any issues with the delivery, we can address those. Then we'll send the next email after they've had the product for a few days, asking what their thoughts on it are. We ask them to share their testimonial in either picture or video form, showcasing how they use the product. We also incentivize them with some kind of discount, offer, or free product to get a testimonial. We test all of those options, but it's pretty well automated through email by now. We also do text messages to get the testimonials as well. Some people will just shoot a testimonial on their phone and text it right back to us. You can't overcomplicate it. A cell phone video is better than a mock-up picture. Any kind of interactive video, even from your cell phone, is going to be a lot better than what you can currently get with still images.

We're heavily eCommerce, and Omnisend is the email marketing and text messaging marketing platform we use inside Shopify. Klaviyo also works great, but it's a bit pared down in comparison. Omnisend shows us the total gross sales amount inside Omnisend, whereas Klaviyo doesn't. It just shows you that it sent an email or a campaign and how much money was made. Omnisend is pretty well priced, too.

WHAT THE FUTURE HOLDS

The CPAs right now are rising not just because of competition, but because you have a lot more people in the field. On top of that, Facebook has cracked down on sketchy advertising. That would be people making false claims or trying to sell things that are fraudulent. The more they crack down on that, the more you'll essentially be priced out of the market. Typically when the Cost Per Acquisition for an order raises, a lot of those people fall off. When you get into those higher CPAs, that's where the real marketers are. If you can get to that point, you have to be ok with what it takes to acquire customers at that level. The strategies to create a higher average value and cover your costs are the difference-makers in Facebook and Instagram ads.

In the future, instead of going for a direct sale, I believe we'll be doing more of a lead generation, such as a giveaway where we have the audience answer questions to win a product. Then we get an email for $0.25 vs. trying to get an order for $25. Once we get an email for $0.25 and we know the person's interested in those products, then we can rely heavily on email marketing in the 30-day lead-up to someone making a purchase and going through the funnel.

Facebook has built-in lead gen features and even has an option for a native lead gen. Use Zapier. It can zap your context directly into a Google Sheet and that Google Sheet can zap it directly into your Omnisend email provider. As soon as it goes into your email provider, it will go into a list and it will go into your emails. You can automate the lead generation coming from Facebook into your email provider and then they go into your email flow.

We have a website called Bless This Farmhouse. We sell everything from barn doors to kitchen sinks. But one product that we're using right now is a bath trough that also has a tabletop, with rustic-looking legs. The product is about $1,000. We have a giveaway where we're giving away one of those every single month. We have a great video of the product and how it works and some great still images of the product. We'll tell people to enter to win. It's pretty simple yet effective for a product where the value is perceived as high. People seem willing to give up their email for the chance to win that.

Now, we do this every single month on every brand because we have almost 400 brands. We're pulling in a ton of leads. Obviously, not everyone wins, and they know that. We have thousands of people who didn't, so it gives us the opportunity to tell them they didn't come in last place. We can tell them they can get the product at a discount because they entered the giveaway. It's another way we spike business for ourselves.

CURRENT TRENDS

We record 1-, 2-, 3-, 4-, and 12-month customer lifetime values. We'll pull all of our customers' total gross spend with us in those time periods and then we'll actually pull that customer data into Facebook--into our advertisements--and we'll set the CPA based on each group's customer lifetime value. That means we're not going to spend more than what that customer is worth to us in that time period on each set campaign. For instance, if someone has already bought from us once, which means we're going to get their second purchase, we need to get that second purchase within the first 30 days. After 30 days, if that second purchase hasn't happened, we're going to pull that ad set and audience out of our advertising.

Understanding the actual dollar amount within a time period that we can track inside Facebook has been essential there. That means understanding how much money has been spent with us. That means understanding the net profit that we made off that customer in a set time period. That profit is the amount of money that we're willing to spend to acquire them. We will go over the amount of money we can get on a customer as well. It depends on how much it's worth for us outside of that 12-month period, as they might not be profitable until the second year.

You can try to leverage software. We do it at scale. There's no software that can do it, but for every order, we do a PNL where we track the order date, the order number, the transaction amount, the vendor cost of goods, and the transaction fees. Percentage-wise, we track the transaction fees per transaction and any refund amounts. We pull those into our total gross order amount, which calculates, through a formula, our percentage of margin. We take that information every single month for each brand, and we'll pull that into a master PNL. We'll determine the amount of gross profit for a month of a particular product or brand, and we'll take our ad spend, software costs, and our labor overhead calculations. That will be our total cost amount, too. Then we can see the gross amount of money we've made. We'll subtract all the other fees, and at the end of the day, we can say whether we are or aren't making money.

(This is why you need to read the bonus chapter at the end with Scott Desgrosseilliers of Wicked Reports.)

I feel like the same things that are working now are going to work long term. Provide great value and great customer service for your customers. Give them a great customer experience and a great shipping experience, and make sure they get their orders fast. If they send an email or a customer service question, make sure you answer them. I think that's what's going to go further than any of the trends or marketing. The moment you get one customer and you understand the customer value, all the other tactics and strategies are nice to try, but the reality is that as long as you serve each customer as a real, individual person, in the long term you're going to be better off. I firmly believe that if you focus on not getting as many customers as possible and instead focus on doing a better job with the customers you get, you can maximize the value of your business or your brand.

EFFECTIVE STRATEGIES

Depending on whether it's a service or a product, the very first thing I would do from a service standpoint is geo-fencing. It is one of the easiest things from a Facebook advertising standpoint, not to mention Google and Bing ads. People are searching for what they need on Google and Bing in certain geographical areas. It's probably the lowest hanging fruit from a marketing standpoint. You just put it within a certain amount of miles in the relevant area and it's a home run. If you've never done marketing in your entire life and you're wanting to get into marketing, make money, and be a business, it's one of the easiest aspects to master. You don't have any kind of strategy behind it besides who you're targeting, the location, and the offer. You can make it better, but it works even at its most basic.

From a product standpoint, the more unique a product, brand, or label that you can create, the more you can differentiate yours from someone else's. It's not so much the physical product itself, but the company, brand, and service that you provide around the product. For instance, Nike, Adidas, and Under Armour all sell shoes, but Nike sells 10 times more tennis shoes. They created a brand around the product. Is a Nike shoe better than a shoe from Under Armour or Adidas? They're all tennis shoes, right? You'll see people debating the merits of each, but in the broader spectrum, they're all tennis shoes that you put on and lace up. It boils down to the brand's customer service, vibe, aura, or the message of what it means to own the product. If you can drive that message home, you'll stop worrying about the actual product itself. That message is what drives the most sales for us. Instead of focusing on selling the product, we focus on selling the type of person that we want to use our product.

To keep track of all of this, we use Google Analytics, Google Trends, Google Keyword Planner, and Facebook Audience Insights. We also use SimilarWeb, SEMRush, and similar software tools to see analytics on companies that are similar to ours.

CONCLUSION

Your Time is NOW! Take Massive Action

Congrats, you made it. You just learned from some of the best Facebook Advertisers on the planet. By doing so, you are now in a position to leapfrog your competition! For this to happen, you have to take massive action. You have to implement or have someone implement them for you. The only way for change to occur in your business to either get you results or prevent results from dipping is by implementing. If you don't, someone else will, and the people that do could be in your industry selling to the same audience.

As mentioned early in the book, E-Commerce is growing. More and more E-Commerce companies are jumping into the picture. This means more and more competition for you. To stave off competition, you have to have and have to keep a competitive advantage. This book gives you that, but only if you take action and implement the strategies in this book. The businesses that take massive action, fast, from this book, will have a competitive advantage.

Facebook and Instagram advertising is also growing with no signs of slowing down. The opportunities to scale your customer list from these two powerful advertising channels are massive and will continue to be massive. Instagram advertising is a channel not to be ignored either. What was once a second thought to Facebook is now a first-thought, especially if your market is prevalent on Instagram versus Facebook. However, as all the book contributors mentioned, you have to tailor your content for each channel to be as effective as possible.

Finally, keep in mind that advertising is just the first step towards getting leads and customers for your business. If you are a seasoned business owner, you already know this. While there are Facebook advertising strategies and tactics that you can implement to get more leads, customers, and sales, cost-effectively, if you don't have a sound website or funnel that converts well, no follow-up, and you don't have monetization strategies and processes in place to maximize the ROI from all your leads and customers, you will struggle at some point. To scale a Facebook ad account to high budgets, you have to have a great business with an optimal average customer lifetime value to afford the higher costs per customer that you will, most likely, incur. That's why the ARM5 Formula and other tips shared by the various contributors in this book could be powerful for you. It all comes down to implementing. Life is short. Don't waste this moment's opportunity. Make 2020 your best year yet in business by taking action, evolving your strategy, improving your tactics, and by implementing them all!

BONUS CHAPTER 1

Karl Schuckert: The Shark of Facebook Messenger Marketing and Founder of Segmate

People call me Karl "The Shark" Schuckert because my background came from the launch industry in marketing. I've helped many startups get off the ground and start making 7 or 8 figures. Because of that background, about 3 1/2 years ago a business partner and I started developing and building a software product called Segmate. It's at segmateapp.com and we are a messenger marketing platform. It's pretty much a full-service platform to help eCommerce businesses, digital marketing companies, local businesses, or anybody with an online presence to capture more leads and communicate better with their audience. I also bring my expertise of marketing into our business. Basically, I teach marketing along with how to use our software.

FACEBOOK MESSENGER ACTIVITY

There are about 1.4 billion active users on Facebook Messenger right now and this number keeps growing every time there's an update. Over 20 billion messages are sent between businesses and customers every single month. People have been neglecting it, but it's finally hitting critical mass and people are starting to accept it more.

You can't ignore it anymore. We firmly believe in email, of course. It's a very viable, old school solution. But we live in an instant gratification world right now. People want answers to things really quickly, and you can't get that with email. Email is very one-directional. It pulls people through with your story, your headline, your subject lines, and your calls to action. Messenger is a little bit different. It's a way of communicating. My background comes from sales and one thing I've always learned about sales is to have a conversation before you sell them something. Provide value to somebody before you sell them something. Email is fairly one way, even though there is a lot of that going on. With Messenger, it has the same feel as a real conversation with somebody, even if you're talking to a bot with predetermined answers. This more conversational atmosphere lowers the trust barriers we have to overcome as marketers to bring in a new client or a new customer into our business. Once people get to know, like, and trust you and your brand enough, they're going to make a binding decision on whether they want to stay or leave.

A lot of eCommerce companies can use it for frequently asked questions. In eCommerce the question usually is about where the product is, shipping IDs, or information along those lines. If you can have the information readily available through a bot it can give people that instantaneous customer service that they want, 24 hours a day and 7 days a week. The other advantage that it does for you, as a business owner, is it puts you closer in touch with your end buyer or end user. That's where things have really started changing. People want to feel close to a company and business. That's why there are still a lot of brick and mortar companies, even with online eCommerce companies thriving. Some people just prefer to go down and talk. Even with businesses closing, there are still major companies that aren't going to go away, like Costco and Trader Joe's. It's because people know that they are going to get that experience when they come in. You want to have that same thing for your customers, but on a virtual level. Messenger and Messenger bots have given you that power.

MESSENGER BOTS AND FRICTION

Messenger bots are still relatively new. Some people feel like Messenger bots haven't proven themselves, but they have. It just takes time. I see so many people in the industry putting in a lot of effort and energy just to use email still. The ones who are actually pivoting and changing are getting a lot more results. Their numbers have gone up. We've helped marketers that sell digital products triple their bottom line numbers and attendance rates on their webinars, plus bring in 40 times more people into their webinar replays. That's just by implementing Messenger into their marketing. People are starting to warm up to the idea. We get trials every single day. It's taken us 3 years to finally get here and get an inch in this space, but we're seeing a lot more people adapting and using it in their businesses and seeing success.

I think the other thing that people have an issue with is thinking that they need to know how to build code. However, a service like ours helps them build it without having to know code. We have all the training at their fingertips, completely accessible to them. It helps people get started and get moving. Even I was lost in the beginning of Messenger bots, but the skills stick with you once you learn them. I still learn stuff here and there. In our software, people are learning something new and rolling out stuff in their Messenger automation all the time. If you're at a higher level and you don't want to do it, hire a service to do it.

STATISTICAL DIFFERENCES

I think having multiple channels is very important. There are a lot of statistics out there. For example, 15%-24% of people will open up an email, whereas anywhere from 30%-90% will open up a message in Messenger. The click-through rates are quite a bit better as well. You have to remember, though, that on Messenger a click is a conversation. It always looks a little bit skewed, as far as the actual clicks to a website or a phone number. I think what would be more beneficial, though, is to talk about some of the ways that you can leverage Messenger that most people don't know.

EFFECTIVE STRATEGIES

There are many ways of opting in. Think of traditional opt-in methods using a web page and a form. If you need to, just Google the term "lead magnet" and find all kinds of articles on lead magnets in marketing. That's the traditional way. You have a high-compelling free offer that has a unique aspect to it, which means the value proposition is very high. The higher it is, the easier it is to get someone to sign up. With the traditional method of taking people to a form, sometimes these forms can be a little bit painful. You're getting a phone number, a first name, a last name, and an email address on one form. Some of them have pre-fill options, depending on your browser, but you're still clicking a lot of stuff just to pass the information. However, Facebook already has all this form data that marketers typically ask for. Roughly 8 out of 10 people are on Messenger and roughly 9 out of 10 people are on Facebook, so they have the typical form data already. They already have people's emails, they already have their phone numbers, and they know even more about everyone, just because almost every website has the Facebook pixel so Facebook is collecting a ton of data on its users.

What Facebook has done is they've allowed third parties like us at Segmate to build around APIs that they've created that give developers access to the Facebook network. A popular feature that we have is called the Send a Messenger button. These are buttons that you can stick anywhere. You can stick them on your store or on your website to get people into your automated Messenger bots. Another popular feature that we have product inside Segmate is called Convert Me, which has pop-ups, sticky bars, slide-ins, and page takeovers. They can pop up after a user-set period of time that someone's been on a user-set page, or if someone tries to exit. Plus, you can stick these buttons on there with videos connected to them or an image with headlines to incentivize them to click the button. When they click the button, we send them a message and as soon as they start interacting with that message they become a subscriber on your list.

Another tool that's really powerful is our checkboxes. You can stick them on buttons or forms on web pages. They even work with popular website building and funnel building tools, like Click Funnels or ConvertTree. They work with all the major builders. As long as they click and check the box on the page, they become a subscriber. We send them a message immediately after that on Facebook Messenger.

Another popular opt-in method is QR codes, which are really good for physical products. This is especially true in cases where you don't know where that person came from. For example, if you're selling on Amazon, Etsy, or Ebay and you control the shipping from your pick, pack, and ship center. Perhaps you are even fulfilling it yourself. Now, what you can do is you can stick a QR code in there with a compelling incentive and instructions to grab a phone, use the camera, and scan the QR code. It works incredibly well with getting subscribers because when they scan the code, it goes to what is called a m.me link. That m.me link opens up Messenger. As soon as they hit the Get Started button they're immediately a subscriber to your Facebook page and you're delivering them something immediately after through a Messenger bot.

Part of the challenge, once someone becomes a buyer of yours, is getting them to become a buyer again. That second buy is so important. You can do it by incentivizing them, such as offering 20%-30% off the next purchase by scanning a code. It's so much better than giving them a website URL on a card because they're probably going to throw it away when they open the box up. If there's a good call to action for them that offers a compelling incentive for them to scan the code with instructions on how to do it, it's going to work out much better to get them to buy a second time.

The m.me link itself is also important. You can stick it anywhere. You could stick it inside the QR code, hyperlink it to blogs, stick it in social media, stick it in PDFs, stick them in images, and so on. Basically anywhere I can stick the link, I can build a Messenger list. That's what we coach users to tell themselves: "Anywhere I can stick a link, I can build a list." If you create a nice post full of value, people will want more information and will click a link in your content. Then, they can join your subscriber base. Then, using automated Facebook Messenger sequences, you can follow up with them in Messenger, just like how you would with email.

Email and SMS are still important, of course. Once they become a subscriber, we have custom input fields. We can use the custom input fields to capture email addresses and phone numbers from their Facebook profile if they have that data inside of Facebook. A high percentage of people, at least, have their email address.

Phone numbers are less common, but you can still ask for people to enter it into Messenger manually. We also have webhooks where you can pass a contact's information through Zapier. Zapier connects software together. With our webhooks, we can send a contact's details to your preferred email marketing service or your preferred text messaging service. We'll send that to them and now you're going to have all 3 follow-up channels started from inside Messenger.

There is also a customer chat widget you could stick on your store or your website. The difference between that and a normal chat widget depends on if you're doing support. I wouldn't recommend this for every page, but on your sales and funnel pages, I do recommend having it. You can handle a sales question right away and you can capture a lead. When people are surfing on your store, that right there lowers barriers of trust. They feel comfortable when they know they can contact you if they need to. You can also customize the message of your chat widget to entice them to click on it and start talking to your chatbot. As soon as they do, they become a Messenger subscriber as well. I recommend using your typical sales questions there. That is key to keeping them on the page and buying your product.

Let's say I'm on my phone looking at some shirts that I want and I start talking to the chatbot, but then I get distracted. Later I go to work and get a message on Facebook that reminds me that I was on the page and asks if I have any other questions. In this example, I had totally forgotten about that. Now I'm going to be able to start talking to them. Facebook also announced that they're coming out with a desktop Messenger app. This means you can get to someone on their desktop or mobile quickly and easily. It's like cross-pollination. As long as you have Facebook and Messenger connected, it's going to be effective.

The next thing is going to be more focused on ads. There are 3 different types of ads you could use. There are a lot of people who go to your store and then leave. You can now remarket to people inside of Messenger and show them an ad inside Messenger. If someone doesn't engage with your message after 24 hours you have 1 more opportunity to send them another message. It can be promotional based, though it doesn't have to be. This is the 24 plus 1 rule. If your content is engaging, you're going to get them to say yes or no before you start selling them something anyway. That's the goal. You want to get them to respond before you show them the promotional part of your Messenger campaign. It resets the 24 plus 1 rule every single time that happens.

If they are outside of that 24 plus 1 rule you can send them an ad that is presented inside of Messenger. Sponsored messages can look like regular messages, but it says "sponsored" on it just like an ad would. It's re-engaging people. You're bringing back old people. You're always still able to bring people back onto your list that you can send messages to. You can also do news feed ads, with Messenger as the objective.

However, if you write something that's very engaging, you have to be careful with page-baiting, engagement-baiting, or comment-baiting. If you create engaging Facebook page content and you include an incentive in it to send your page a message, every single person who clicks on the button in the post will get what we call a non-subscriber message sent to them. As soon as they open up that non-subscriber message and start engaging with your bot, they become a subscriber. Then you can incentivize them to share that post as well in their group. If they're sharing your content that's valuable to them, it's a good way to get very inexpensive exposure.

There are a few other strategies out there but those are the main ones that I see people using. We build strategies around those main ones. It's also threefold, as Facebook doesn't just send you a message in Messenger. When you get a message sent to you they also send you an email and push notifications. They will even send text messages, if that option is turned on by the contact.

If you're just getting started in all of this, the best way is to use segmateapp.com. There's a 14-day free trial there. If you feel like you want to get in for training you can go to buildabotcourse.com. There's also 1000bot.com. You have options so you can dive in and start using Facebook Messenger automation to grow your business.

BONUS CHAPTER 2

Scott Desgrosseilliers: The Advertising ROI Optimization Master and Founder of Wicked Reports

The father of modern advertising said, "Half my marketing is wasted. I just don't know which half." There's no excuse for that nowadays with tech, the right approach, and the right framework. You can know which marketing's working and which is wasted, and that fuels marketing attribution. Being able to sort that all out happened to be a unique talent I had.

Here's the story: I had a client called Get Maine Lobster who was trying to target people who didn't live in New England but liked the Patriots or Red Sox, and to see if they would become customers or not. There was nothing that existed that could help that size of a business with advertising attribution to a sale, so I hacked something up by using Microsoft Excel and pivot tables. Then more and more people kept coming in just by word of mouth from what I was doing for Get Maine Lobster. I created Wicked Reports out of my own personal need to make it easier to maintain the reports I had to generate for people. It turned into a much bigger venture than I originally envisioned.

WICKED REPORTS

I was doing some Infusionsoft consulting from 2012-2014 with random, complex technical projects. It was always some sort of integration project for people using Infusionsoft. A friend of mine from Get Maine Lobster explained that Facebook wasn't working for his niche. He spent $4,000, got 12,000 clicks, and only made 1 sale for $200. When I asked him if he thought eventually some of those people would buy, he had no idea how to predict that. That's how it all started. After 3 months, I was able to tell him it was women aged 40 or older who liked the Patriots or Red Sox but didn't live in New England and were worth $10-to-$1 in 3 months. It blew his mind. While initially he was reluctant to do paid advertising at all, now he does multi-channel paid advertising. He reports about $3 million in revenue from those channels. That's $3 million from channels that he was not even going to use. I didn't even know to call it marketing attribution at the time. That was the beginning of doing ROI tracking, pre-Wicked Reports. Then, one-by-one, as questions kept coming and as others started using my process, it slowly evolved into the Wicked Reports of today.

In its most basic sense, marketing attribution is determining what is working and what's not working. You do that by connecting your marketing spend to clicks, to actual leads, and to actual sales. Other places use statistical models and sample your data, and then make inferences, or take ad platform data as is. But in general, it's just trying to figure out where you should spend your money and where you should stop spending your money.

We're going multi-channel because a lot of ad platforms, particularly Facebook, will take credit when your email might have closed the sale. That's a negative aspect of ad platforms compared to how we measure it more truthfully. We also start from conversions that happen in your CRM or Shopping Cart and look back in time, whereas ad platforms take a click and look forward in time. It's just a different way of looking at it. We like our way because we're starting from really high-value conversions and high-quality data signals. If you spend based on them, you're more likely to make money, though that's not to say that a Facebook conversion or a click somewhere in your funnel wasn't important. We found that this approach works best. We can verify it and you can trust it.

Another big thing with us is that for people either making sales over the phone or with subscription businesses, we're wired in and can report those sales back against Facebook or Google ad spend. That's where we can show you more ROI when they may not. We can do that automatically with our technologies that we've built now. If you get a lead and it takes 2-3 months to close, then when everyone's looking for more leads like those, we know which leads have led to the highest customer lifetime value. We show that in our reports so you can spend intelligently more there, based on your best customers and the highest customer lifetime value.

We take an inbound click from Facebook and track what happens with that person, basically forever. Now, Facebook's giving us the cost data for your campaigns, ad sets, and ads, so we use the cost data but that's all we use. We then rely on your CRM to tell you if this person became a new lead or if they opted in for some marketing because they were already on your list. That's a re-engagement of an existing prospect. Brand awareness really affects how different campaigns are going to work at different points in the funnel. It is usually more likely that a campaign that works at the top of the funnel on your cold traffic is not the same type of marketing that's going to show at the bottom of the funnel when you're trying to close them. Our attribution models take that into effect and are always considering that interaction with your brand when we're trying to classify where someone is in your funnel automatically. Now, with Facebook, you would set up those conversions yourself and then report them in. They're still going to be anonymized, but on Facebook, all we rely on is how much you have spent. Then we're putting an identifier on the link so we know which ad they clicked on during the customer journey. From that point, we take over and we don't rely on their data for much other than occasionally using it for view attribution.

A simple example of the difference between Wicked Reports and the Facebook Ads Manager would be to look at a typical Shopify store. On the 'thank you' page, you have the Google conversion code, you have the

Facebook conversion code, and you might have Pinterest or Snapchat or another conversion set up. Imagine someone comes to your store and converts. Imagine you're showing ads on all 4 channels and successfully getting people to click on or at least look at your ads, and then someone clicks off one of your Infusionsoft emails and buys. If you look at all of those ad platforms, they're all going to show a conversion possibly based on your settings. If you added them all up, you might see that you had 5 sales that day. Really, you only had 1 sale and all the ad channels took all the credit. That's the worst-case scenario. It's not that you don't need to get their conversion codes in place, because that's still giving them data and helping to optimize for results on their platform. Sometimes, ad platforms can track micro-conversions that are not sales but are still very important steps. You should still do that. We're only focused on marketing attribution of who deserves the most credit for the most important parts of your customer journey in a way that you can make mathematical sense of.

ADVANTAGES OF WICKED REPORTS

If you're not a household name, there's a particularly big advantage for brands that either have subscriptions or their leads take time to buy. We provide a lot of value in figuring out what campaigns found the leads to begin with that became the highest-valued customers. We have a specific section of a report called Missed Opportunities where we call out where you've turned off your ad spend but the leads are still buying. We'll create a report for it for a particular attribution model related to new lead generation results. Then, we'll see that there's revenue there even if you're not spending ad spend. We see a lot of big results where people turn back on campaigns that they didn't realize were working. The hardest thing to swallow is finding cold traffic leads that become high-value customers from inactive campaigns.

Not that all of it isn't hard, but retargeting already warm traffic is a little easier to do than just going off cold and inviting someone in. People succeed at it, but it's like the 80/20 rule. You have to test a bunch of stuff and find out what works. You're having this challenge of time until they're going to buy so you're evaluating that in the ad platform. From there, you won't see the sales conversion data that you're looking for. You might lose faith because you can't just spend in the face of uncertain ROI or no ROI. A lot of our successes are around providing clarity there.

For instance, we were the first company to partner with Google on putting top and middle funnel lead conversions automatically into their platform with dollar values, so their smart campaigns will automatically adjust the bids based on which search campaigns at the top or middle of the funnel are actually leading to the sales downstream. Google's algorithm already tries to do that, but the better the data it has, the better the results it will get. With one client, it was about a 1900% increase in his performance. Google is tricky and you have to let their algorithm machine-learning learn. It's hard to let it learn when you want to tweak the campaigns that aren't working. Well, he turned it on, went on vacation, and just crushed it. We have 1 or 2 really advanced marketers who are used to tweaking things constantly and hyper-segmenting. There's nothing wrong with that approach if it works, but if you have a smart campaign with particularly smart bidding choices, you need to let it learn and you need to let it make adjustments over a couple of weeks.

It's not that the marketer's job is going to be taken by bots and algorithms, but it's changed. It's more about your response to testing offers, ad copy, hooks, and feeding it proper data, then analyzing the data when there have been enough results. If you get no results, you can kill a campaign, but you want campaigns to have enough spend to have enough conversions so that the learning can take place. Rather than having 10 campaigns at $10 each, it's better to have 1 campaign at $100. It depends on your market, but you need conversion data and you need it fed in. Google and Facebook are both the same in that regard.

If you don't have a lot of budget, you need to work on 1 funnel and worry about getting that dialed in instead of doing dozens of different things. As you get started, you're going to get something that's making sales and then determine if you have enough data that you can analyze it. Then, you can start making data-driven decisions to scale results. If you have a small number of sales, your data's going to tell you that you need to do better. You need to actually get some volume in. That's when you get more and more data-driven. At the start, you want to be data-driven as much as you can, even if it's just Google Analytics. You need to have ideas of what you want to try, what you want to move forward with, and how long you want to do it for, rather than constantly adjusting things. You should be constantly testing ad creative, but if you don't have a framework for how you're going to analyze your data to make decisions, you're just going to be aimlessly clicking around looking at pie charts and graphs. You need to have a goal when you're looking at the data.

MAXIMIZING ROI WITH WICKED REPORTS

I would pick 3 things. First is our attribution. We need to make it user-friendly and understandable because if you don't understand or act on the data we're showing you, you're going to stop paying us. We have a vested interest in doing that, but that's also the reason we exist: so you can understand and act on the performance data.

What we do is map the attribution models to specific marketing strategies, new lead gen, re-engaging existing leads, and how to get awareness in a new market. It means you can evaluate your campaign performance the correct way rather than trying to become an attribution model expert without any guidance.

Everyone's trying to find new leads that become great customers. That attribution model is called First Opt-In, which is about what marketing you did that led to someone being created in your CRM for the very first time. That's what creates a new lead. All of a sudden, you have a new contact. Ideally, it becomes more than that and becomes a paying customer, but the only way to properly know if someone is a new lead is to be wired into your CRM and make sure when they're clicking, they weren't already on your email list. Otherwise, they are an existing lead which is then more familiar with you, and that's a much bigger commitment on the way towards the buying journey. We map these different attribution models based on how we plan to use them specifically. For example, what creates new leads. You can pick First Opt-In and we have training for things like how to measure new leads and why. We will show you the new leads of that campaign. You can click on them, see who they are, and see the date of the click, the date of the Opt-In, and the date of the purchases.

Secondly, when we're attributing the revenue of the orders, it's based on real orders. You can see the order IDs on what they purchased. You can then filter out certain products to see the ROI on them against your marketing spend. Furthermore, you can click through and see the entire customer's past clicks and the journey of every individual customer. You're not going to do that if you have a couple thousand customers a month, but for your highest value of customers, you can get a feel of what their type of journey is. You can see their landing pages, ads, results, and orders or no orders if they didn't buy. Whatever it is, you can see the whole journey rather than just trusting that we've rolled up the data correctly. We're a customer data platform, as well, just by the nature of what we do. People love looking through past clicks particularly because we won't match Facebook's data. Otherwise, we'd get you to use Facebook. When we don't, people like to see why not. Generally, that's because either we're attributing that marketing somewhere else, like Snapchat on the top of the funnel, or because we're showing more revenue because we've connected into your order systems. If the order took longer than you'd like but it's still attributable back to a Facebook or Instagram click, we can show that value. People like the fact they can see everything and trust it.

Everyone wants great ROI and the question becomes, once you have enough campaigns running, should you scale? Are you doing better or worse than normal? The only way to know that is to know your benchmarks based on what you were trying to achieve in the campaign and how long you were doing it. You can't say you want new leads that buy and expect it to work like magic. If you run a campaign and your leads normally take 3 weeks to buy, you can't be sweating the performance after 2 days. You've got to give it a fair amount of time. You also need to know if the trend is matching how you normally do it so you know when it's better to be patient or not. To this point, we built in benchmark reporting based on your historical performance so you would know the time it takes for leads to buy. There's another report that shows these benchmark averages for companies around the same size. You can see if you're doing better or worse than normal based on the goal of that marketing campaign.

You've got trend lines for cost and revenue. If they start to even out, you realize you're running out of fish to catch with a particular ad set. You may need to stop. There are a lot of indicators and training around how to use the benchmarks because it's a big thing when you're running all this data. There are 3 main things to decide with the data: scale, kill, or chill. The chill, deciding if it's alright to relax a campaign, is the toughest part. The cleaner and more accurate your data is, the more you can chill. That's why our customers love Wicked Reports.

ACKNOWLEDGEMENTS

Publishing a book, whether it's your first or second time, takes discipline, determination, and hard work. The first book was harder to get to the finish line than this one but this one still took focus and discipline to get to the finish line. Luckily, I wasn't doing this alone and have created invaluable strategic partnerships with partners that have helped me realize my dream of publishing this second book. Special thanks to Aaron Wang and his team at Writers Cartel for your support. In addition, special thanks to Kelly Exeter for helping me get the book to the finish line. Thank you so much for your work here.

I'm also honored to have some incredible contributors this time around. I still pinch myself that I'm associated with some amazing entrepreneurs and that I live the life I live. Special thanks goes to these folks for contributing invaluable contributions to this book: Jason Hornung, John Hutchison, Cody Neer, Nehal Kazim, Jeremy Howie, Rory Stern, Jeremy Wainwright, David Schloss, Enrico Lugnan, Phil Graham, Mari Connor, Karl Schuckert, and Scott Desgrosseilliers. Finally, I also want to thank the team at CVO Acceleration for helping to design the exterior of the book, for supporting me as I worked on the book, and for driving the book's success at launch.

Finally, the idea of a family of books came from two people: Adam Lyons and Brian Kurtz. Adam, our conversation spawned the first book. I'll always be grateful. Brian, you validated the idea that I had in my head to turn the first book into an on-going series. You validated the long-term strategic impact that this could have. Thank you!

Finally, in no particular order, thank you for helping and supporting me at some point during my 7+ year Entrepreneur Journey:

Brenda Mendez, Oli Billson, Rich Thurman, Devolis Newburn, Rodney Hearns, Scott Oldford, Ryan Deiss, Richard Lindner, Kendra Wright, Joanna Ulloa, Justin Walsh, Jennifer Kem, Ben Thompson, Tahnee Lynch, Daniel Joseph, Ian Erlandson, Dirk Littrell, Kelsey Bratcher, Dustin Young, Josh Stockton, Greg Hickman, Adam Sell, Tim Falcone, Valerie Falcone, John Mikan, David Gonzalez, Gonzalo Paternoster, Ryan McKenzie, Shannon Hernandez, Josh Stepenenko, Curt Maly, Andrew O'Brien, Sean Whalen, Joe Polish, Earnest Epps, Shawn Byrnes, Rudi Ornelas, Jason Valasek, Joshua Valentine, Nicholas Bayerle, Kathy Buchanan Yturralde, Mike Gelblicht, Karl Schuckert, Todd Brown, Kevin Donahue, JimmyTay Trinh, Nick Cirello, Aurelijus Terminas, Trish Sanderson, Nicholay Okorokov, Kamila Zamaro, Vikki Mattera, Emerita Salvador, Khalid Essam, Sophie Gambet, Adrian Carrales, Lola Acheampong, Michael Zhang, Marisa Tusha, Jek Tibayan, Nick Silikov, Markus Heitkoetter, Pat Johnson, Dave Albano, Ross Walker, Damian Rufus, Raven Kleinbach, Daryl Hill, Jaime Masters, Daniela Moreno, Jesus Diaz, Leticia Diaz, Dornubari Pope Vizor, David Nguyen, Kraig Kubicek, Jeremy Montoya, Vin Featherstone, Jonathan Khorsandi, Kathy Goughenour, Tony Martin, Mike Morelli, Dan Martell, Michael Lovitch, Hollis Carter, Joshua B Lee, John Lee Dumas, Freddy Lansky, Michael Keefrider, Kate Erickson, Navid Moazzez, Jamal Miller, Kevin Breeding, James Schramko, John Dennis, Esther Kiss, Jon Schumacher, Arjun Brara, Heather Ann Havenwood, Katya Sarmiento, Brian Bargiel, Russell Lundstrom, Kristina Rueling, Jesse Elder, Jon Morrow,

Ron Reich, Charl Coetzee, Phil Randazzo, Greg Reid, Dennis Yu, Brian Kurtz, Diana Lane, Brandon Campbell, Lain Ehmann, Wes Schaeffer, Ted Miller III, Guillaume Couillard, Chris Mercer, Valerie Viramontes, Grant Andrew, Adan Perez, Sarah Laws, Jay Patel, Ian Garlic, Jay Fiset, Ivan Glushko, Uli Iserloh, Caitlin Pyle, Brian Johnson, Jeff Nabers, Rachel Nabers, Victoriya Scovel, Tony Tovar, Austin Iuliano, Chad Collins, Justin Christianson, Daniel Rose, Chris Lee, John Davy, Allen Brouwer IV, David Rice, Troy Salewske, George Macrodimitris, Henry Gridley, Aaron Wiseman, Adrian James, Richard Cussons, David Littrell, Luke Pawlikow, Alexander Willoughby, Kara Pierce, Scott Desgrosseilliers, Chandler Bolt, Ryan Levesque, Rachel Wilmann, Craig Dewe, Jovan Will, Fernando Godinez, Richard Miller, Chen Yen, Andy Hussong, Pat Flynn, Graham English, Tony Alfreda, Kimberly Bean Holmes, Rob Holmes, Jon Marino, Zach Johnson, Ian Stanley, Peter Bragino, Guido Bonelli, Janet Beckers, Rob Hegarty, Phly Jambor, Michell Corr, Ed Wotring, Justin Rondeau, Christian Burris, Ian Nagy, Chase Frost, Chip Baker, Michael Hunter, Jacki Mclenaghan, Lisa Schulteis, Melodie Moore, Carrie Lynn-Rodenberg, Deborah Hanchey, Scott Wells, Piyush Parikh, Kevin Mogavero, Ed O'Keefe, Roland Frasier, Tommie Powers, Dobbin Buck, Cory Snyder, Justin Sandy, Mikal Abdullah, Jess Wilkinson, Josh Wilkinson, Zach Obront, Jayson Gaignard, Debra Stangl, Rachel Kersten, Greig Wells, Lynika Cruz, Chuck Trautman, Kim Snider, Charlie Lyons, Monaica Ledell, Lea Rosa Garcia, Christian Bonilla, Kevin Johnson, Patrick Phenix, Dominick Sirianni, Meghan Alonso, Marc Mawhinney, Niel Issa, Janet Issa, Bret Thomson, Garrett Cannon, Sophia Bera, David Bullock, Nikki Black, Chris Higbee, John Howell, Wardee Harmon, Robert Michon, Michael Anthony, Angela Kerr, Gene Morris, Andrea Hale, Joel Young, Andrew Warner, Ethan Sigmon, Kim Phillips, Josh Turner, Chris Danilo, Nick Jensen, Adam Teece, Lawton Chiles, Regina Bellows, Russ Henneberry, Nolan Nissle, Kathy Lane, Burhaan Pattel, Mark Bailey, Michael Mathewson, Ryan Farrell, Chris Copp, Jet Berelson, Tamsin Silver, Chris Plough, Peter Li, Carlos Alvarez,

Jeanna Pool, Roger Miller, Katie Miller, Shane Smith, Jenny Holla, Robyn Jackson, Tyler Bramlett, Jennifer Patterson, Tracy Matthews, Lindsey Yturralde, Alecia Smith, Scott Vogel, Matt Esaena, Scott Voelker, Tabitha Armstrong, Lisa Kuecker, Erika Rodriguez, Candy Rodriguez, Becky De Acetis, Phil Costantino, Jake Spear, Kimberly Najarro, Ricky Baldasso, Ben Cummings, John Allen Mollenhauer, Nicole Munoz, Ron White, Michelle McGlade, James Roper, Colin Morgan, John Belcher, Justin Brooke, Geeta Sidhu-Robb, and, last but not least, the Next Level Business Scale family, the Digital Marketer family, the Infusionsoft Partner community, Superfast Business, and the Baby Bathwater community.

Most importantly, I want to thank my family, Mom, Dad, Bob, Rachel, Laney, Cody, Roscoe, Kobe, Nickel, and my son, Ben. My family has always stood by me through the toughest moments of my life to date. I love you guys with all my heart. To my son, without you, I not only wouldn't have become an Entrepreneur and now an Author, but I would have never become the man that I am today. You are the future and will rise. Keep pushing yourself to your potential.

STAY IN TOUCH

If you have any thoughts or comments that you'd like to share with me about the book, please email me at josh@joshmarsden.com.

I would also recommend that you head on over to joshmarsden.com and watch The E-Commerce Performance Marketing Show. This 100% free show is dedicated to E-Commerce businesses and designed to help you scale your company with powerful tips, interviews, strategies, tactics, and more.

You can also follow me at:

- Facebook: facebook.com/joshmarsden
- Instagram: @joshuaamarsden
- LinkedIn: linkedin.com/in/joshmarsden

If you appreciated the value and hard work that went into this book, I would love if you were to tag me on Instagram with a photo of you holding this book. I'll give you a free $10 gift card to Amazon for doing so. Plus, it would really make my day!

Keep in touch!

Josh Marsden, MBA